THE GREAT SCUTTLE

THE END OF THE GERMAN HIGH SEAS FLEET

WITNESSING HISTORY

DAVID MEARA

AMBERLEY

In memory of Winnie and Leslie Thorpe

First published 2019

Amberley Publishing
The Hill, Stroud,
Gloucestershire, GL5 4EP

www.amberley-books.com

ISBN: 978 1 4456 8700 1 (print)
ISBN: 978 1 4456 8701 8 (ebook)

British Library Cataloguing in Publication Data.
A catalogue record for this book is available from the British Library.

Typeset in 10pt on 13pt Celeste.
Typesetting by Aura Technology and Software Services, India.
Printed in the UK.

Contents

Preface

The story of the scuttling of the German High Seas Fleet in Scapa Flow on 21 June 1919 has been told in a number of books and the outline of events is not in dispute. Even so, there must be many people who have barely heard of this extraordinary drama which took place in a remote location well after the end of the First World War. In June 2019 we commemorate the centenary of the greatest single loss of shipping in maritime history, an event that made a profound impression on those who witnessed it happen. None of those witnesses are still alive, but many left written and verbal accounts of what they saw, often recording in vivid detail their impressions of the drama and confusion of that day. I have a personal interest in the subject because my mother and uncle were two of the party of Stromness schoolchildren on the deck of the *Flying Kestrel*, being taken around the German fleet on a sightseeing trip when the scuttling began and the big ships began to turn turtle all around them. My uncle left a detailed account of what he saw, and this gave me the idea of telling the story of that day using as much eyewitness material as I could find. I hope that these on-the-spot accounts, together with a wealth of images, both historic and contemporary, will bring this event alive with vividness and immediacy, as we commemorate the scuttling 100 years after it took place on that glorious Midsummer's Day in Scapa Flow.

Acknowledgements

The definitive account of the history of the Royal Navy leading up to and during the First World War is *From the Dreadnought to Scapa Flow* in five volumes by Arthur J. Marder. The final volume, published in 1970, gives an authoritative account of the surrender and scuttling of the German High Seas Fleet. Two earlier books, *The Story of Scapa Flow* by Geoffrey Cousins, 1965, and *Scapa Flow* by Malcolm Brown and Patricia Meehan, 1968, include a number of eyewitness accounts from those still young enough to recall in vivid detail what they saw at the time. Then, in 1986 Dan van der Vat produced a detailed narrative, *The Grand Scuttle*, which included the results of his researches in the West German Federal Military Archive in Freiburg. This is probably the most comprehensive narrative of the German fleet from its creation to its disgrace and annihilation that is still in print. Other books which include accounts of the scuttling include *This Great Harbour: Scapa Flow* by W. S. Hewison, 1985; *Scapa: Britain's Famous Wartime Naval Base* by James Miller, 2001; and *The Ships of Scapa Flow* by Campbell McCutcheon, 2013.

I am grateful to the staff of the Orkney Library and Archive in Kirkwall and to the staff of the Stromness Museum for their kindness and help; to the staff of the Image Sales Department of the Imperial War Museum and the Picture Library of the National Maritime Museum, Greenwich; Alamy Ltd; the National Museums of Scotland; the Harris Museum and Art Gallery, Preston; Bridgeman Images; Nick Gribble; and for personal information and help from Patricia Beauchamp, Sheena Taylor, Leslie and Joyce Howard, Garry Gibson, Sandra Rodwell, Zona Paton, and Stephen Harwood. I would also like to thank Radio Orkney and the *Orcadian* newspaper for their help in tracking down eyewitness accounts, and Connor Stait and the staff at Amberley Publishing for their continuing help and support. I would like to thank Tracey Salt for typing the manuscript and Melinda Cole and Ken Taylor for technical assistance with the images. For the encouragement and support of my wife Rosemary, without which this project would not have been completed, I offer my heartfelt gratitude and love.

21 June 1919: A Day to Remember

Leslie and Winnie Thorpe
with their mother Elizabeth,
a photograph taken in 1919.
(Author's Collection)

A nine-year-old girl and her older brother stood at the window looking out across the still waters of Scapa Flow. Their house, Melvyn, was perched on the hill halfway up Hellihole, the quaintly named lane that led from the winding main street of the fishing port of Stromness up to Brinkies Brae, the hill that rose up steeply behind the little grey town. Consequently, they had a fine panoramic view across the vast stretch of water that had formed the anchorage for the British Grand Fleet during the First World War, and which was now the place of internment for the German High Seas Fleet while the Allied Powers wrangled over its fate at the Peace Conference at Versailles. Over the previous seven months Winifred and Leslie Thorpe had become accustomed to the sight of these German warships as they swung at anchor around the islands of Cava and Fara in the parts of the Flow called Bring Deeps and Gutter Sound. They had become part of the everyday scenery, a source of wonder and curiosity for the schoolchildren of the town. The German ships had been anchored there since late November 1918, enduring the rigors of an Orkney winter, slowly rusting and becoming ever more bedraggled and unkempt. But on this Midsummer's Day of 1919 the schoolchildren of Stromness Academy had been promised the privilege of a boat trip across the Flow to view these ships at close quarters. So on this particular morning Winifred and Leslie were full of excitement and anticipation, especially as, after two stormy days, Saturday 21 June dawned bright and clear, with blue skies and

A contemporary photograph of Melvyn House, showing Leslie and Winnie Thorpe and their parents standing by the garden wall. (Author's Collection)

Melvyn House, Hellihole Road, Stromness, the home of Leslie and Winnie Thorpe, from where they watched the German fleet in the Flow, and set out to board the *Flying Kestrel*. Note the two harbour lights, on which ships would align themselves when entering Stromness Harbour. (Author's Collection)

The view down the Flow from Stromness Academy, above the town of Stromness, with the lighthouse on the island of Graemsay in the middle distance and the island of Hoy on the far right. (Author's Collection)

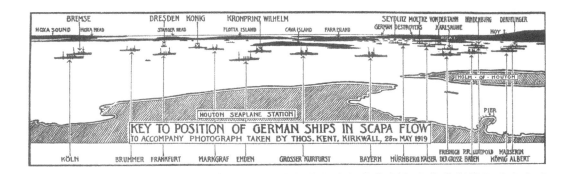

The German fleet at anchor in Scapa Flow. A view taken from above Houton Naval Air Station. An accompanying key identifies each of the German ships. (Stromness Museum)

very little wind. It was a perfect day for such a treat, and they were both up and dressed in good time, ready to join their schoolmates and gather at the pier to board the boat that was going to take them around the Flow. As they gazed out of the window, eagerly discussing the day ahead of them, they could have had no idea just how exciting and momentous the events of that Midsummer Day would prove to be, a day that they would remember for the rest of their lives.

CHAPTER 1

Surrender

Scapa Flow is a great natural harbour, a body of water about 120 square miles in area, encircled by the Mainland of Orkney and the southern isles, and strategically placed off the north coast of Scotland with easy access both to the Atlantic Ocean and the North Sea. The islands of Orkney, in the words of John Tulloch, whom we shall meet later on in this story,

A view across the Loch of Stenness to Stromness, with the hills of Hoy in the distance, on a beautiful summer day. (Author's Collection)

can be as bleak and dreary as any place in the world when the western gales blow in from the wide sweep of the Atlantic Ocean or the blizzards of snow beat down from the Arctic Circle in the dead of winter when the hours of daylight are short and the sun sends forth no warming rays. But the springtime can be a season of soft western breezes, the lengthening evenings mellow with the call of nesting Lapwings, the perfume of fresh seaweed on the skerries and the song of the sea on the cliffs a continual roar that has a melody of its own: The summer a haze of primroses and blue lupines, the enchanting song of the skylarks on the endless days that hardly know any darkness, the fogs of May that bring the Arctic Terns so mysteriously can clothe the islands in a mantle of romance that calls to mind the Viking Long ships of yore.

Communities had lived around Scapa Flow in the Stone, Bronze and Iron Ages, and the Vikings used the Flow as a raiding base as early as the seventh century AD. They named it Scapa from a Norse word meaning 'isthmus', which refers to the strip of land between the town of Kirkwall and Scapa Bay. Later on, in 1263, King Hakon of Norway gathered a large fleet of war galleys there for his doomed campaign to subdue the Scottish mainland.

Over subsequent centuries the Flow was used in the naval campaigns of the seventeenth and eighteenth centuries and by the ships of the Hudson's Bay Company, but it began to be used as a naval base by the Royal Navy in 1812, during the Napoleonic Wars, and two Martello towers remain on either side of Longhope as evidence of the Admiralty's interest.

The eastern end of Scapa Flow on a clear summer's day, looking across to Burray and South Ronaldsay with Flotta over to the right. (Author's Collection)

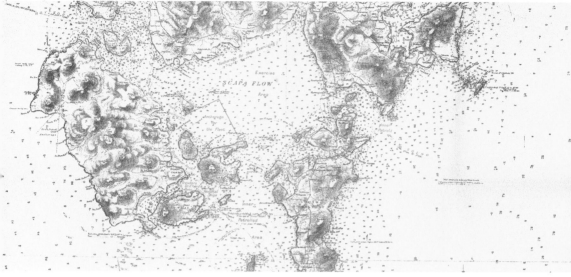

A contemporary naval chart, showing the Orkney Mainland and southern islands, with the anchorage for the Grand Fleet outlined in red, the exercise area and the location of fleet auxiliaries, destroyers and hospital ships. (Author's Collection)

During the years leading up to the start of the First World War there was considerable debate about the strategic value of the Flow as the base for the Royal Navy. Winston Churchill, as First Lord of the Admiralty, felt it was too far away and would have preferred the Firth of Forth, but as time ran out it was agreed that Scapa Flow should form the fleet anchorage, even though its defences were weak, and measures were taken to make improvements.

Admiral Viscount Jellicoe of Scapa, in his book *The Grand Fleet*, published in 1919, commented that during November 1914 the work of sinking blockships in all the main entrance channels to Scapa Flow, except the Hoxa and Hoy entrances, was carried out, although the lack of cement ballast and the strong tides rendered the work of blocking only partially effective. In addition, coastal defence batteries were built, and boom defences and nets were stretched across the entrances to prevent enemy submarines getting into the Flow. In 1914 the main base headquarters was at Scapa Pier near Kirkwall, but this was subsequently moved to Longhope, and the fleet was moored off Flotta.

In spite of its primitive defences, and continuing doubts about its suitability as the main fleet base, Scapa Flow remained the anchorage for the British Grand Fleet throughout the First World War. From here the fleet sailed in May 1916 to engage the German High Seas Fleet in the Battle of Jutland, and shortly afterwards Lord Kitchener, the Minister of War, sailed in HMS *Hampshire* on his fateful mission to Russia. The ship struck a mine off Marwick Head at Birsay during a gale and almost the entire ship's company lost their lives. The monotony of life in the Flow was briefly relieved by visits to the fleet by the Archbishop of York in June 1915 when he held a huge open-air service on the island of Flotta, and in June 1917 when King George V visited the fleet and toured the flagships.

Towards the end of 1916 Admiral Jellicoe had been made First Sea Lord, and Admiral David Beattie became the new Commander-in-Chief of the Grand Fleet. He was a more

H. M. King George V, Admiral Sir David Beatty and Commander Viscount Curzon on board the battleship *Queen Elizabeth* in Scapa Flow, 22 June 1917. Curzon appears to be holding a camera to record the visit of the King. (Imperial War Museum Photographic Archive)

swashbuckling figure who wanted to keep fleet morale high, in spite of the fact that the enemy refused to leave its base at Wilhelmshaven. Moreover, Beattie preferred Rosyth on the Forth as a strategic location for his ships, and from April 1918 he made it the main fleet base. Although there was still round-the-clock activity in Scapa Flow, the focus of naval operations had moved further south. Thus it was that when the Armistice was declared, which stated that the German High Seas Fleet would be interned until the Allied Powers could decide on its final disposition, it was from the Firth of Forth that the Grand Fleet set out to rendezvous with the enemy and escort them to their final destination – Scapa Flow.

On 21 November 1918 the British light cruiser *Cardiff*, with the 6th Light Cruiser Squadron, led the German fleet from the Heligoland Bight across the North Sea to the rendezvous point about 40 miles east of the Firth of Forth. 370 British ships, with 90,000 men, sailed out in line ahead to open water and then, following the details of 'Operation ZZ', they split into two lines 6 miles apart, with Sir David Beatty's flagship HMS *Queen Elizabeth* last in line. The warships were cleared for action in case of last-minute treachery by the Germans. The *Cardiff* led the German High Seas Fleet in single line ahead, nine battleships, five battlecruisers, seven light cruisers, and forty-nine destroyers, between the two British lines. The Allied ships then turned and reversed course, and on either side

13

The light cruiser HMS *Cardiff* leading the German High Seas Fleet to surrender in the Firth of Forth on 21 November 1918. The *Cardiff* is leading the German fleet in a single line between the lines of Allied warships, according to a carefully choreographed plan designed to emphasise the might of the Allied navies and to humiliate their vanquished foe. Oil Painting by Charles Dixon (1872–1934) (National Maritime Museum, Greenwich)

A panorama of the surrender of the German fleet on 21 November 1918, showing HMS *Cardiff* leading the German battlecruisers, flanked by HMS *Lion* and HMS *Queen Elizabeth*.

of the German line proceeded towards the Firth of Forth in silence, and at 11 a.m. the entire armada anchored in the Forth. On Beatty's orders the German ships hauled down their flags. It was a moment of humiliation for the German sailors, but one of triumph for the Allied Powers. Witnessing this, Admiral Chatfield wrote:

> The surrender of the German Fleet was to many of us a highly painful if dramatic event. To see the great battleships come into sight, their guns trained fore and aft: the battlecruisers, which we had met under such very different circumstances, creeping

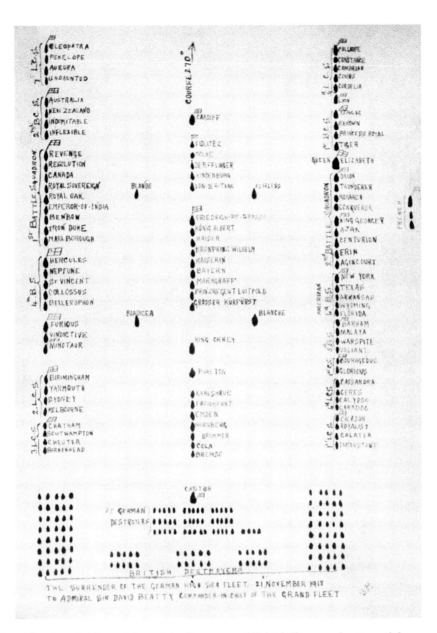

The chart showing the disposition of the German and British fleets at the time of the surrender on 21 November 1918. This carefully choreographed plan brought the German High Seas Fleet, led by the cruiser HMS *Cardiff*, between the rows of Allied warships, demonstrating the might of British naval forces and their supremacy over their enemy. (Imperial War Museum Photographic Archive)

towards us as it were with their tails between their legs, gave one a real feeling of disgust ... Surely the spirit of all past seamen must be writhing in dismay over this tragedy, this disgrace to all maritime traditions.

(*The Navy and Defence*, London, 1942)

British battlecruisers performing their manoeuvre to turn and escort the German High Seas Fleet to Rosyth on 21 November 1918. (Imperial War Museum Photographic Archive)

Hand-painted china bowl presented by Colonel Henry Halcro Johnston to mark the octocentenary of St Magnus Cathedral, Kirkwall, 1937. It is painted with scenes of the surrender of the German High Seas Fleet, and in an oval panel is the signal of Admiral Sir David Beatty: 'The German flag is to be hauled down at Sunset today and is not to be hoisted again without permission. 21st November 1918'. (Orkney Islands Council)

NAVAL SIGNAL.

		P.O. OF WATCH	
		READ BY	
FROM	TO	REPORTED BY	
		PASSED BY	
C. in. C. Grand Fleet	*Grand Fleet.*	LOGGED BY	
		SYSTEM	*W/T*
		DATE	*21/11/18.*
		TIME	

It is my intention to hold a Service of Thanksgiving at 1800 today, Thursday, for the victory which Almighty God has vouchsafed to His Majesty's Arms and every ship is recommended to do the same   1255

C in C Grand Fleet to Admiral Von Reuter. The German Flag is to be hauled down at 1557 today, Thursday, and is not to be hoisted again without permission.   1450.

Naval signal from Admiral Beatty. Pasted into the back of Claude Leaney's diary are copies of various signals which he had received as the telegraphist, including this one from Admiral David Beatty, received at 12.55 p.m. on 21 November 1918: 'It is my intention to hold a service of Thanksgiving at 1800 today, Thursday, for the victory which Almighty God has vouchsafed to His Majesty's Armies and every ship is recommended to do the same.' Later in the afternoon at 1450 pm the following signal was sent: 'C in C Grand Fleet to Admiral Von Reuter. The German Flag is to be hauled down at 1557 today, Thursday, and is not to be hoisted again without permission.' (Orkney Photographic Archive)

The meeting and mingling of these two great fleets was an unforgettable sight, the British Grand Fleet dominating and outnumbering the German ships in a well-orchestrated gesture of victorious supremacy.

Claude Tennyson Leaney was a telegraphist on board HMAS *Melbourne,* a light cruiser of the Australian navy, which joined the Grand Fleet in 1916 in the North Sea and performed mine-sweeping and patrol duties based at Rosyth and Scapa Flow. He kept a detailed diary and recorded the events surrounding the surrender:

Thursday 21st November *"DER TAG"* anchored at Rosyth. We weighed at 3 am and with rest of LCS proceeded out of harbour astern of the 3rd LCS. We were followed by the remainder of the Grand Fleet in two lines on our way to meet the German High

Surrender of the German High Seas Fleet, 21 November 1918. (Oil Painting by Bernard Gribble) This is one of a number of paintings depicting the momentous day when the German Fleet surrendered. Gribble shows the scene from the deck of the USS *Texas* as Admirals William Sims and Hugh Rodman of the US Navy watch the line of German warships move into position. (Bridgeman Images)

Seas Fleet who were to surrender to us off May Island. Three ships of the 6th LCS had gone out to meet the German Fleet to lead them up the Firth of Forth. We sighted the leading German ship at 9 am and were steaming past them shortly afterwards. The first batch were 5 Battlecruisers and 9 Battleships, behind them came 7 Light Cruisers followed by 49 destroyers. The 50th destroyer V30 was mined and sunk on the way across. The German ships for internment were:-

Battleships	Battlecruisers	Light Cruisers
1. *KAISER*	1. *MOLTKE*	1. *NURNBERG*
2. *KAISERIN*	2. *SEYDLITZ*	2. *EMDEN*
3. *MARKGRAF*	3. *VON DER TANN*	3. *BRUMMER*
4. *BAYERN*	4. *DERFLINGER*	4. *BREMSE*
5. *FRIEDRICH DER GROSSE*	5. *HINDENBURG*	5. *FRANKFURT*
6. *KONIG ALBERT*		6. *KARLSRUHE*
7. *PRINZ REGENT LUITPOLD*		7. *COLN*
8. *GROSSER KURFURST*		
9. *KRONPRINZ WILHELM*		

* An American Lieutenant, a German Interpreter, came aboard us on arrival. He is here for operations tomorrow.

cancelled. 'Patriot' made special trip to Rosyth with urgent case for hospital and returned at 3pm, bringing our mails back with her. We weighed at 8pm and proceeded up harbour. Fog lifted. We anchored in C3 berth at 10pm. *

* **Thursday 21st November.** "DER TAG." Anchored at Rosyth. We weighed at 3am. and with rest of 2nd L.C.S. proceeded out of harbour astern of the 3rd L.C.S. We were followed by the remainder of the Grand Fleet, in two lines, on our way to meet the German High Sea Fleet who were to surrender to us off May Island. Three ships of the 6th L.C.S. had gone out to meet the German Fleet to lead them up the Firth of Forth. We sighted the leading German ship at 9am and were steaming past them shortly afterwards. The first batch were 5 Battlecruisers and 9 Battleships, behind them came 7 light cruisers followed by 49 destroyers. The 50th destroyer "V 30" was mined and sunk on the way across.

The German Ships were the

Battleships		Battlecruisers	Light cruisers
1. MOLTKE.	4. DERFLINGER	1. KAISER.	6.
2. SEYDLITZ	5. HINDENBURG.	2. KAISERINE.	
3. VON DER TANN.		3. MARKGRAF.	
		4. BAYERN.	
		5. FREIDERICK DER GROSSE	

A page from the diary of Claude Tennyson Leaney, who served as a wireless telegraphist in the Australian warship HMAS *Melbourne*. He travelled with his ship all over the world, including a spell of patrol duties at Scapa Flow and as part of the escort at the surrender of the German High Seas Fleet. This page of the diary describes 'Der Tag' when the Allies met the German ships off the Firth of Forth. (Orkney Photographic Archive)

1918.

The German Ships for internment were:—

Battleships	Battlecruisers	Lightcruisers
KAISER	1. MOLTKE	1. NÜRNBERG.
KAISERIN.	2. SEYDLITZ.	2. EMDEN.
MARKGRAF.	3. VON DERTANN	3. BRUMMER.
BAYERN.	4. DERFLINGER	~~BREMEN~~
FRIEDRICH DER GROSSE	5. HINDENBURG.	5. FRANKFÜRT.
KONIG ALBERT		6. KARLSRUHE.
PRINZ REGENT LUITPOLD.		7. COLN.
GROSSER KURFÜRST.		4. BRELISE.
KRONPRINZ WILHELM.		

with 49 destroyers. The Coastal Airship N.S.8. flew over us at 9.30 am and headed for the German Fleet and was flying over the leading battlecruiser when she passed out of sight in the mist. We were level with the German Light Cruisers and turned about at 10 am. and headed for Rosyth. We passed May Island at 1.45 pm. We anchored at 3.20pm abreast the German Fleet, their light cruisers being between us and their battleships & Battlecruisers, on the other hand were the German destroyers surrounded by about 300 of ours. The 2nd Line & the 1st B.S. ie. "Iron Duke," "Emperor of India", "Benbow"

"Marlborough", anchored to seaward of the German Fleet. The 2nd BCS ie. "Australia" "New Zealand", "Indomitable" & "New Zealand", and anchored to seaward of the Battleships, the 3rd LCS anchored outside of us. Our Grand Fleet made a Signal to Admiral Von Reuter, of German Fleet, that the German Flag was to be hauled down at sunset and not to be hoisted again without special permission. At 5pm boarding parties from different ships went aboard the respective German Ships, for which they are detailed, for a cursory examination of Guns, ammunition, Torpedoes and war- heads. The German ships carried 10 rounds a gun, the fuses were taken out and confiscated by the boarding parties, they returned aboard at 6.30pm leaving final examination till tomorrow. Thanksgiving Service was held in the wreck at 6pm.

Friday 22nd November. Anchored off Inchkeith in Firth of Forth. We commenced coaling at 8.30 am. Our Boarding Party went aboard the "Nürnberg" at 9am for a thorough inspection of Stores etc. We finished coaling at 10 am having received 210 tons. Boarding party returned on board at 11.30 am. We learned that 18 of crew of "V30" had been sent ashore

A page from the diary of Claude Tennyson Leaney, a telegraphist on HMAS *Melbourne*, listing the German ships sailing into internment, and describing the events of 21 November 1918. He mentions that the airship 'NS8' flew over them at 9.30 a.m. Later they sent boarding parties onto the German ships to check that they were fully disarmed. (Orkney Photographic Archive)

With 49 destroyers. The Coastal Airship NS8 flew over us at 9.30 am and headed for the German Fleet and was flying over the leading battlecruiser when she passed out of sight in the mist. We were level with the German Light Cruisers and turned about 10 am and headed for Rosyth. We passed May Island at 1.45 pm. We anchored at 3.20 pm abreast the German Fleet, their light cruisers being between us and their Battleships and Battlecruisers, on the other side were the German destroyers surrounded by about 100 of ours ...

A German perspective on the event was given by Friedrich Ruge, at that time in command of one of the torpedo boat divisions. He described in his book *Scapa Flow 1919* what it felt like as the German fleet was met off the Firth of Forth by the full might of the Grand Fleet:

There they came in the poor light of a grey November morning and surrounded us from all sides – squadron upon squadron and flotilla upon flotilla. In addition to the 40 British capital ships, there were almost as many cruisers, 160 destroyers, an American squadron, a French ship and also aircraft and small non-rigid airships. Everywhere the crews stood by the guns ready for action equipped with gas masks

HMS *Cardiff* leading the German fleet to surrender, 1918. (Watercolour by Charles Dixon) The frame bears a longer inscription: 'H.M.S. Cardiff leading ships to surrender, as seen from HMS *Seymour*. Nov 21 1918 Time 10.45 am. Distance at sea about 30 miles.' The artist has taken some license in depicting what would have been a line of ships at greater distances from each other. He includes the naval airship 'NS8' (top right corner), which was aloft with 'NS7' filming the event for the newsreels. 373 mm x 520 mm. (National Maritime Museum, Greenwich)

An aerial view of the *Friedrich der Grosse*, the German flagship, leading two Kaiser class battleships into Rosyth. Taken from the airship NS7 or 8, which were filming the surrender for the newsreels. (Imperial War Museum Photographic Archive)

Friedrich Ruge (1894–1985) was an officer in the German Imperial Navy and Officer Commanding the destroyer SMS *B 112*, which was interned in Scapa Flow. He was instrumental in scuttling his ship, and wrote about his experiences in the book *Scapa Flow 1919: The End of the German Fleet*, published in England by Ian Allan in 1973. The picture shows him later in his career as chief of minesweepers in discussion with other officers on exercise at sea, 1939. (Alamy Ltd)

and flame-proof asbestos helmets. If the situation was depressing for us, the deployment of such over-whelming strength looked like a grudging recognition of the former power of the High Seas Fleet.

I had the morning watch. Our boats proceeded in five parallel lines behind the long column of the big ships. Every line was led by a British destroyer and the whole by a light cruiser of the 'C' class. These fast and, for their size, very powerful ships with their fine, sleek lines at once aroused unqualified admiration.

The Times correspondent watching from the deck of the British flagship HMS *Queen Elizabeth*, wrote in awestruck terms:

The annals of naval warfare hold no parallel to the memorable event which it has been my privilege to witness today. It was the passing of a whole fleet, and it marked the final and ignoble abandonment of a vainglorious challenge to the naval supremacy of Britain.

In a letter to his uncle written from HMS *Royal Sovereign* on 27 November, Lieutenant Commander Henry Harwood described the arrival and inspection in the Firth of Forth:

'In honour of the British Navy'.
A print by Sir Bernard Partridge
commemorating the surrender of the
German High Seas Fleet. From *Punch*,
27 November 1918. (National Maritime
Museum, Greenwich)

My dear Uncle Harry

A few lines to tell you about the Hun Fleet.

We left Rosyth at 2am last Thursday and the Fleet formed up in two lines. The Huns were led in between us and we turned and steered for the Firth of Forth. On arrival at Rosyth the Germans were anchored in their billets and we anchored all round them.

The next item in the programme was an inspection to see that they had no ammunition or torpedoes onboard. The Commander, Gunnery Commander and myself (Torpedo Officer) went over and did this. The next day we all went over again with a large number of assistants to carry out a more detailed inspection. Both showed no signs of explosives which was satisfactory. It really was a most extraordinary proceeding. We went alongside in our Picket Boat and were piped over the side in the usual manner. We were received by several of their officers. Their men were all aft smoking and lounging on the Quarter Deck.

They have on board what they call "Members of the Soldiers and Workmen's Council". They wear white and red bands on their arms. The officers have to get all their orders signed by the Council but once they are signed the officers have full power to carry them out. On the whole there is still quite a lot of discipline left but the men seem to spend all their time smoking on the Quarter Deck.

Needless to say we were very formal. Grave salutes and no shaking of hands etc and only strictly business remarks were passed. We were treated quite courteously and especially so by the Men. It is very hard to understand but I can't help thinking that the Hun sailors think they are on our side against their officers. For instance the Men were much more inclined to show us details of the ship than the officers were. Their ships were filthy and can't have been painted for years.

I forgot to say the ship we had to inspect was the *Kronprinz Wilhelm* – or in other words *Little Willie*. I hear in one case that the Captain and First Lieutenant both burst into tears. I am not surprised; I should hope it was with pure shame. How the German Navy could have managed to give itself up without a fight passes my comprehension. It is a poor reward for us after all our labours to simply have to herd in a lot of sheep.

Beatty addressed the officers and men of the 1st Battlecruiser Squadron on 24 November just before it left the Firth of Forth:

They are now going to be taken away and placed under the guardianship of the Grand Fleet at Scapa, where they will enjoy, as we have enjoyed, the pleasures of Scapa. [Laughter]. But they have nothing to look forward to as we had … They have nothing to look forward to except degradation.

Between 25 and 27 November the ships steamed northwards to Scapa Flow, their place of internment. Admiral Franz Von Hipper had resigned as Commander of the Fleet rather than surrender his ships, delegating the task to Rear-Admiral Ludwig Von Reuter. He had the unenviable job of coaxing his often mutinous crews to obey orders. Their mood of anger and shame was summed up by Seaman Richard Stumpf of the dreadnought *Heligoland,* as recorded in his diary entry of 24 November 1918:

Vice-Admiral Ludwig Von Reuter (1869–1943) from a photograph taken in 1920. When Admiral Franz Von Hipper refused to lead his ships into internment, Von Reuter was asked to take command of the German High Seas Fleet. He was responsible for ordering the scuttling of his ships, as a result of which he was made a prisoner of war, and only released in 1920. On his return to Germany he was greeted as a hero who had rescued the honour of his navy and the German people.

I wish I had not been born a German. This despicable act will remain a blot on Germany's good name forever ... Although our army is still much respected by foreigners, the actions of our High Seas Fleet will live on with shame in history.

Lieutenant Commander Henry Harwood continues his letter with a description of the events of the journey northwards and the arrival in Scapa Flow:

All the inspections being satisfactory they left in batches for Scapa Flow, each batch being led and escorted by a division of the Fleet. We left Rosyth yesterday at noon with 4 Huns (*Bayern, Markgraf, Kronprinz Wilhelm* and *König Albert*) astern of us and the remainder of our division astern of them.

We arrived here at Scapa at 9 am this morning after an uneventful trip. Our Navigator at once went on board and took them to their internment billets. I don't think they will get away easily now. Even if any escape they will only get onto Orkney Island so they can't do much harm. Meanwhile I fear we have to stay in this beastly place watching them.

Thomas Young, a Marine Corporal based at the shore battery at Houton on the Mainland of Orkney, described their arrival in Scapa Flow from the shore:

They came in one long line and as they came nearer I could hear their bands playing lively music, which I thought was very funny. They must have been just as pleased as we were that all was over. They all dropped anchor more towards Hoy but near

SMS *Emden, Frankfurt* and *Bremse* entering Scapa Flow to begin their internment in November 1918. (Imperial War Museum Photographic Archive)

enough to see quite plain with the naked eye. As each ship was put in place the bulwarks were soon crowded with men fishing. It was very comical, but they might have been hungry. After a few days big liners began to arrive and took the crews off the ships and back to Germany.

As the German ships arrived, the destroyers and other small craft were moored in pairs in Gutter Sound between the islands of Hoy and Fara, and the battleships and cruisers were moored to the north and west of the island of Cava. Their wireless apparatus was removed, their guns immobilised, and most of the crews were repatriated back to Germany after three weeks. Of the 20,000 German sailors who arrived in Scapa Flow, only 5,000 remained. The British ordered that the maximum strengths of the crews remaining on board should be:

200 for battlecruisers
175 for battleships
60 for light cruisers
20 for torpedo boats

Friedrich Ruge described what he saw as he arrived in the Orkney Islands:

> The region did not appear very enticing as we entered. Under a grey sky there were bare islands of rock, covered only here and there with undergrowth and heather, a few huts, many sheep, very few humans, and great swarms of seagulls and cormorants in the air and on the water. These were the main impressions. Nor did we gain many others in the course of the internment. A low-lying rock in the middle of the bay looked at first sight like a whale. The British called it 'the barrel of butter'.
>
> The entrances were protected by booms and nets and were guarded by numerous small vessels. In the southern part of the bay a British battleship squadron lay at anchor – our guard. An officer came on board as harbour pilot and indicated where our torpedo boat division's berths were: two mooring buoys in the western part of

The German battlecruiser SMS *Hindenburg* at anchor in Scapa Flow. (Imperial War Museum Photographic Archive)

A pair of German destroyers, possibly *G 101* and *102*, moored in Gutter Sound, Scapa Flow. (Imperial War Museum Photographic Archive)

The interned German fleet with HMS *Carlisle* and HMS *Blonde* in Scapa Flow. (Watercolour by William Wyllie) (National Maritime Museum, Greenwich)

the bay between the islands of Fara and Risa. *BI10* and *BI12* formed one 'bunch' and *BI09* and *BIII* the other.

Immediately in the vicinity of the group *BI09/BIII* was the buoy for the British guard destroyer, a little too near for our taste. It quickly made itself unpopular by completely suppressing the excursion traffic which soon began with the dinghies to our good friends in neighbouring flotillas.

So ended this extraordinary movement of ships into captivity in all but name, with strict orders that there should be no communication between the vessels, and that no-one was to be allowed ashore. Wireless apparatus was removed, thereby isolating the Germans from events in the outside world and leaving them in ignorance of the negotiations going on at the Peace Conference. The Germans were prisoners on their own vessels, their mood a mixture of demoralisation and indiscipline.

After the Battle of Jutland in 1916 the German High Seas Fleet remained in harbour, and the ships' crews became disillusioned with the progress of the war and the German monarchy. Secret sailors' councils were formed on a number of ships, and in October and November there were serious disturbances and open mutiny at Kiel and Wilhelmshaven. Over the coming months this mutiny spread across the country with workers' and soldiers' councils being elected, modelled on the Soviets of the Russian Revolution of 1917, which took over power in many cities.

Because of the revolutionary upheavals at Kiel and Wilhelmshaven the German Fleet had sailed under the Red Flag, with sailors' committees on board whose cooperation the officers relied upon to run the ships. The result was that no maintenance was done, and conditions became indescribably filthy. Food was sent from Germany twice a month but was monotonous. During the long, dreary days the sailors lounged about the decks, smoked, and caught fish over the side of the boats. Post was infrequent and censored, and although there were doctors within the German fleet there were no dentists, which sometimes led to chronic tooth decay and associated complications.

John Tulloch, born in Burray and reared on a farm on the island of Cava, retained vivid boyhood memories of the arrival of the German fleet in the Flow, because the biggest ships were moored in an arc around the western end of the island.

To the west lay the SMS *Seydlitz, Moltke, Von der Tann, Hindenburg, Derfflinger* on the outside line and the SMS *Nurnberg, Kaiser, Kaiserin, Prinz Regent Luitpold, Baden* and *Bayern* on the inside line. After that they curved around the Calf of Cava until they reached the Barrel of Butter; a small reef with a navigation light on it, practically in the dead centre of Scapa Flow. My home stood near the shore on the west side, therefore the battleships that I have named became an everyday scene to me as the months went past, in fact some of them were so near to my home that on a calm day we could hear sailors talking or singing quite clearly. On a Sunday a brass band on the SMS *Friedrich der Grosse* used to play their German military tunes when the weather was good, so those great ships became a part of my childhood days, a source of jetsam that was picked up on my wandering around the shore of my island home.

Christmas came and the German crews, though far from home and virtually prisoners in their own ships seemed to enjoy themselves as best as they could.

We could hear them larking around the decks of the SMS *Nurnberg* and *Kaiser*, the ships nearest to my home. They sang Christmas carols, but their songs sounded strange and guttural to our ears. When Christmas was over they must have thrown all their memories of it overboard because many weird things to my young eyes floated ashore on the western seas. Small Christmas trees and their decorations, acorns, coloured electric globes, Christmas cards and letters written in beautiful longhand – all a great source of wonderment to me.

SMS *Grosser Kurfürst* taking up her moorings in Scapa Flow in November 1918. (Imperial War Museum Photographic Archive)

The German fleet, a view taken from Houton Seaplane Station. (Author's Collection)

Admiral Von Reuter recorded his own impressions of this remote northern anchorage:

The internment weighed on us all. Still, what comradely friendship could not give us, and what the hate of the enemy could not rob us of, was the wonder of nature at Scapa Flow.

The scenery around us was really harsh and desolate. And yet this forgotten corner of the Earth had its attractions, its beauty – not by day, during glaring sunlight or when the rainclouds painted everything grey on grey, but in the evening or by night. Then it was that the Northern Lights would cast their rays like searchlights over the clouds and light them to a yellow hue, then again pour themselves over the whole firmament in a single sea of fire ... the clouds were fired and in their flaming fire rose the dark, naked cliffs of the mountains of Orkney – There is yet a God!

Von Reuter exercised overall command from the battleship *Friedrich der Grosse*, with the use of a British drifter to visit his ships, but he had to transfer his flag to the light cruiser *Emden* because of indiscipline and insubordination among the troublemakers on his flagship. In a letter to the Admiralty he stated:

During the second half of December disturbing influences began to make themselves noticeable in a few ships, especially *Friedrich der Grosse*. Political agitation became intense. A small group terrorised the whole flagship. A number of men under the leadership of a stoker petty officer were responsible for these excesses.

SMS *Emden*, which became the flagship of Admiral Reuter, moored in Scapa Flow. (Imperial War Museum Photographic Archive)

Because of this agitation, and to make his management of the crews easier, over the period of nearly seven months' internment the number of men under his command was continually reduced, to 5,000 by the end of the year, with further reductions to under 2,000 by June 1919.

Von Reuter early on decided in view of what he felt were the very severe conditions of the Armistice and the failure of the Allies to honour their obligations, that 'the enemy himself paved the way for the scuttling'.

Article 31 of the Armistice declared: 'No destruction of ships or of materials (is) to be permitted before (their) evacuation, surrender, or restoration.' Although no British guards were posted on the ships, armed trawlers and drifters constantly patrolled the anchorage on the look-out for any signs of sabotage. The British were certainly aware that scuttling was a possibility, and with good reason.

It is possible that Von Reuter left Germany with the understanding that the ships were to be destroyed rather than surrendered. As early as January 1919 Von Reuter discussed with his Chief of Staff the possibility of scuttling the fleet, and in May he began laying firm plans to do so, having learnt that the final peace terms would require the surrender of the entire Fleet. After the final crew reductions on 17 June 1919, Von Reuter circulated orders about scuttling his ships to all his commanding officers: 'The Commanding Officers are ordered to make the necessary preparations for sinking their ship so as to ensure that on receipt of the order she will sink as rapidly as possible.'

German battleships and light cruisers at Scapa. (Watercolour by William Wyllie) (National Maritime Museum, Greenwich)

Paragraph 11 of the orders stated:

It is my intention to sink the ships only if the enemy should attempt to obtain possession of them without the assent of our government. Should our Government agree in the peace terms to the surrender of the ships, then the ships will be handed over, to the lasting disgrace of those who have placed us in this position.

Meanwhile, at the Peace Talks there was considerable dispute among the Allied nations about the disposal of the German fleet, the Italians and French hoping to incorporate some German ships into their fleets, while the Americans opposed adding any ships to the British fleet as this would exacerbate Anglo-American rivalry. As the discussions dragged on Admiral Wemyss expressed the British viewpoint in a note to the Deputy First Sea Lord:

You and I know what an embarrassment it would be to us to have any of these German ships, and you and I know that we should like to see them sunk, but I do see that they are a pawn in the game.

This view was echoed by the Prime Minister, Lloyd George, who expressed the view that all the German ships should be towed into the middle of the Atlantic, surrounded by all the ships of the Allied nations, 'and to the music of all their national anthems be ceremonially sunk!'

A König class battleship at anchor in Scapa Flow. Members of the crew appear to be fishing over the side. (Orkney Photographic Archive)

In fact the British had already laid plans to seize the German ships at midnight on 21/22 June to forestall any subversion. This was approved by the Admiralty, who nevertheless neglected to inform Vice Admiral Sir Sydney Fremantle, Officer Commanding the 1st Battle Squadron, which was guarding the German Fleet in Scapa Flow, that the deadline for signing the treaty had been extended until 23 June. Fremantle only saw this in a newspaper, and assumed that it was true. As Fremantle had been under orders for some time to take the British battlecruiser squadron out on exercises, he decided that the weather during the night of 20 June was sufficiently favourable, and he ordered the squadron to prepare to go to sea at 9 a.m. the next morning, 21 June. Fremantle and Von Reuter subsequently disagreed about whether the latter had been informed that the Armistice was still in effect. Whatever the truth, the fates seemed to have conspired to present Von Reuter with the perfect moment to scuttle his fleet and save his country's honour. As Friedrich Ruge recalled in his account of the event, 'June 21st brought marvellous spring weather with radiant sunshine, clear air and no wind. Scapa Flow was for once really beautiful. The only thing that did not harmonise with all this was the fact that it was a critical day of the first order.'

Winnie and Leslie Thorpe, standing at their window that summer morning looking down the Flow, were completely unaware of all the frustrations, humiliations and confusions of the previous seven months. Apart from any gossip they had picked up from the conversation of their parents and teachers about the German fleet, they had become

Admiral Sir Sydney Fremantle (1867–1958). Fremantle had an active naval career during the First World War, commanding several cruiser squadrons. He was promoted to Vice Admiral at the end of the war and given command of the First Battle Squadron. He was responsible for guarding the interned German fleet in Scapa Flow, but had taken his squadron to sea on torpedo exercises on 21 June 1919.

The German fleet anchored in Scapa Flow, taken by Thomas Kent on 28 November 1918. (Author's Collection)

accustomed to these enemy ships and viewed them as a somewhat mysterious and alien presence alongside the smartly turned out ships of the Grand Fleet. Today, however, was an exciting opportunity to get close up to them, to identify some of these great battleships, and see the sailors who remained on them. Full of excitement, Winnie and Leslie made their way to Stromness Academy, where they joined their schoolmates in the playground. It was going to be a day to remember...

CHAPTER 2

Scuttle

Stromness Academy, showing the buildings as they were in about 1915 with children making their way up Franklin Road to school, and playing in the playground. (Orkney Photographic Archive)

Leslie Thorpe's diary for Saturday 21 June 1919 begins: 'Went down to see the German Fleet. Everyone came to school about 9.45 am and we marched to the *Flying Kestrel*, which was at the New Pier.' *The Flying Kestrel* was a tug from Liverpool, used to supply water and general stores to the British ships in Scapa Flow. The crew list as recorded in 1915 was headed by Thomas Davies, aged fifty-eight, as Master, together with a crew of twenty-one, including three engineers, ten firemen, five able seamen, two stewards and a cook. Many of the crew came from Liverpool, and only a handful were native Orcadians.

The Stromness Senior School classes (i.e. secondary and upper primary) were being taken on the trip, leaving behind the Infants, and they marched down to the pier in class order, between 200 and 300 children in all. Leslie Thorpe gave further details of the day both in his diary and in a long letter which he wrote to his father two weeks after the scuttling:

> The *Kestrel* was quite big enough to hold us, and we had liberty to go almost all over her. We had the Red Ensign at the stern, the Union Jack at the bow, and the pennant with the ship's name at the fore-mast-head. We passed through the hurdles

Leslie Thorpe's letter, written to his father on 6 July 1919, describing the events of 21 June, and his trip on the *Flying Kestrel*. (Author's Collection)

The *Flying Kestrel*, a tug used to take water and supplies to the British fleet. Originally registered in Liverpool, and with a number of crew members from Liverpool, it was the boat on which the Stromness schoolchildren set sail to tour the German fleet on the morning of 21 June 1919. This photograph shows the *Flying Kestrel* at Stromness with the children on board. (Orkney Photographic Archive)

'The German Fleet Caged in Scapa Flow' by William Lionel Wyllie (1851–1931). Wyllie was a marine artist with a passion for naval battles, who wrote books about the sea battles of the First World War. Here he depicts the German fleet at anchor in the Flow with the boom and net defences in the foreground. (National Maritime Museum Greenwich)

[Part of the anti-submarine defences which included nets and booms and sunken blockships across the main entry and exit channels: fishing nets were hung from buoys and strung across Hoxa Sound and Hoy Sound until stronger defences were put in place.] and the first German ship we came to was the *SMS Baden*. She is a battleship, having two masts, and two funnels close together, two big guns aft, and two forward. The next was the battlecruiser *König Albert*. The battlecruisers all have very pointed sterns, and their names are at the stern instead of at the bow. They have the Kaiser's name on each side, thus:-

W

II

The next ships were the battle cruisers *Kaiserin, Derfflinger, Hindenburg, Von der Tann, Moltke* and *Seydlitz*. I never noticed the *Kaiser* or the *Karlsruhe*. Perhaps I wasn't looking when we passed them.

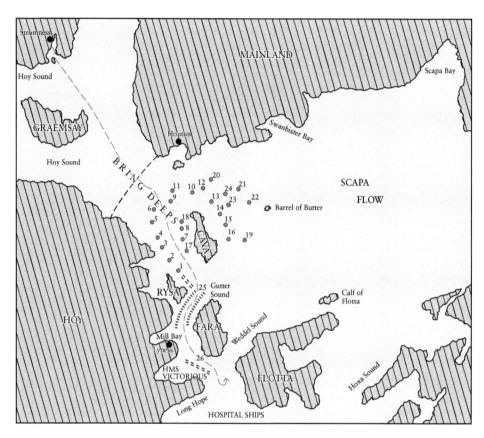

Map showing the position of the interned German High Seas Fleet in Scapa Flow before the scuttling on 21 June 1919, and the route taken by the *Flying Kestrel* through the German fleet. (Author's Collection)

Key:
Broken line in black – Boom Defences
Broken line in red – Route of the *Flying Kestrel*

Disposition of German fleet: 1) *Seydlitz*; 2) *Moltke*; 3) *Von der Tann*; 4) *Hindenburg*; 5) *Derfflinger*; 6) *Kaiserin*; 7) *Kaiser*; 8) *Prinzregent Luitpold*; 9) *König Albert*; 10) *Friedrich der Grosse*; 11) *Baden*; 12) *Bayern*; 13) *Grosser Kurfürst*; 14) *Kronprinz Wilhelm*; 15) *Markgraf*; 16) *König*; 17) *Nürnberg*; 18) *Karlsruhe*; 19) *Dresden*; 20) *Emden*; 21) *Frankfurt*; 22) *Cöln*; 23) *Bremse*; 24) *Brummer*; 25) Destroyer flotilla; 26) Destroyer flotilla.

From Leslie Thorpe's narrative it is clear that the *Flying Kestrel* sailed south through the part of the Flow known as Bring Deeps and between the lines of the larger German ships lying to the west of the island of Cava. Although they passed very close to the German ships, the children had been given strict instructions not to signal or wave to the German sailors. Instead they were encouraged by the Headmaster Colonel Hepburn to hold a competition to recognise and record as many of the names of the interned ships as they could. Peggy Gibson, a schoolgirl on the *Flying Kestrel*, recalled that it was only when they were sailing down the Flow that they were told that the British battle squadron had left for torpedo exercises in the Pentland Firth. The children were disappointed, but there was more than enough to occupy their attention as they sailed past the German battleships and cruisers, and through the lines of destroyers moored between Rysa and Fara. Leslie Thorpe picks up the story again:

> These ships lay two or three side by side. We saw two or three British destroyers, the *Westcott* among them. Then we came to a British battleship HMS *Victorious* [the base flagship]. We passed a floating dock and HMS *Imperieuse* ... We kept on our way past Lyness where we saw a railway engine running along a light railway. We went on further so as to see two hospital ships *Berbice* and *Agadir*. They were beautiful. Then we turned back intending to go home round the other side of Cava to see the other ships ...

The light railway engine at Lyness noticed by the young Leslie Thorpe, a railway enthusiast, as he travelled down the Flow in the *Flying Kestrel*, from *Scapa and a Camera* by C. W. Burrows, London, *Country Life* 1921.

Hospital ships at Scapa Flow. (C. W. Burrows)

The *Flying Kestrel* was at this moment steaming northwards up Gutter Sound. Captain Davies and his crew had remarked on the absence of the British fleet and found it strange that the Flow was virtually empty of Allied warships. After circling round the *Cyclops*, the depot ship, the *Flying Kestrel* began its journey back to Stromness, and had travelled about a third of the way through the German fleet when for the schoolchildren their sightseeing trip suddenly became much more exciting than they could ever have imagined.

At 9 a.m. that morning the 1st Battle Squadron of the Royal Navy weighed anchor and steamed out through Hoxa Sound, bound for torpedo practice in the Pentland Firth. When they had gone, all that remained to guard the German Fleet was the flagship *Victorious* under the command of Vice-Admiral R. J. Prendergast, Officer Commanding Orkney and Shetlands. The destroyer HMS *Westcott* was refuelling at Lyness and the destroyers *Walpole* and *Vega* were under repairs at the Depot Ship HMS *Sandhurst*.

Admiral Von Reuter had already distributed his orders about scuttling around his fleet to all his commanding officers, with its crucial Paragraph 11. After reading a report in *The Times* of 16 June 1919, Von Reuter had concluded that the Armistice would come to an end at midday on 21 June. He claimed that Admiral Fremantle had neglected to inform him that the date for signing the Treaty had been postponed for two days, and when he was told that the British battle squadron had left harbour for the open sea, he realised that his moment had come. He gave the order for the pre-arranged signal to be sent for the ships to be sunk: 'Confirm Paragraph 11: Commander Internment Force.'

Friedrich Ruge, in command of the torpedo boat division, describes how an order came from the Admiral to prepare for 'Pennant Z', a forked red flag which was the torpedo boats' attack signal. His account continues:

In order not to leave anything undone, I once again checked for myself that everything was ready below for immediate flooding. Then I put on the clothes which lay ready with two thicknesses of underclothing and packed washing and shaving

HMS *Cyclops*, a fleet repair ship, at Longhope. From a drawing in *Scapa and a Camera*. (C. W. Burrows)

Vice-Admiral Sir Robert John Prendergast (1864–1946). Portrait Painting by Francis Dodd. Son of a Surgeon-General, Prendergast entered the Navy in 1877, was promoted to lieutenant in 1887, trained as a gunnery officer, was promoted commander in 1899 and in 1901 became Captain of HMS *Excellent*. In 1911 he was appointed Captain-Superintendent of Sheerness Dockyard. In November 1914 he was promoted rear-admiral, and in May 1916 he was appointed Rear-Admiral Commanding Scapa Flow, hoisting his flag on the depot ship HMS *Victorious*. In 1919 he became Vice-Admiral Commanding Orkneys and Shetlands, and retired in 1920 with the honour of Knight Commander of the Order of the Bath.

material with a few handkerchiefs and collars in two small packets which I could stick in my pockets, if necessary. When these preparations were completed, I went on *BIIO*, where a few stragglers were still breakfasting, made some jokes about the unmistakable tension and proved that there could be no scuttling on June 21st. Then we went on deck to enjoy the sun.

Suddenly there was a cry, "Call from *Seydlitz!*" Involuntarily we looked in her direction to read the signal. There, on this battlecruiser, which lay nearest us, several men were running at top speed along the deck. We had never seen anyone running on a big ship in Scapa. So something must be wrong.

Simultaneously *S138*, the command boat of the leader of the torpedo boats, hoisted 'Pennant Z'. So it was already starting!

The strange feeling that the great moment had now come did not last long because there was a lot to do. The flotilla commander briefly communicated the order to scuttle the boats to the officers and crew members near him. Then we all went to our stations and what followed went according to plan.

The technical personnel opened the valves and the covers of the condensers and smashed the pipes which had been previously earmarked. The sailors hoisted the ensign, the commanding officer's pennant and 'Pennant Z'. Then they opened the hold-covers, the cabin doors and portholes, immobilised the anchor capstan and threw all equipment overboard which might serve to free the boat.

Admiral Reuter had issued the preliminary order to stand by at 10 a.m., with the order to scuttle about an hour later, but it naturally took some time to be passed around the fleet and for a response to be sent back. At about 11.30 a.m. acknowledgements began to arrive back at the *Emden*, but Reuter had held back giving the order to scuttle to his own flagship, because there were two water boats alongside, which would have been alerted by the excitement and activity that something unusual was happening. However at about 12 noon, according to Reuter's account, the *Friedrich der Grosse* was seen to be listing, and her boats were being lowered. In his order of 17 June Reuter had stipulated in Paragraph 4:

If possible not more than one boat – for rescuing the crew – is to be cleared away ready for lowering. A flag of truce is to be prepared to take away in the boat. The boats with the crews on board are to make for the nearest land: they will remain together under the orders of their officers.

Following these orders Friedrich Ruge on the destroyer *BIIO* ordered his men into the cutter and they rowed to the nearest island.

Nine-year-old John Tulloch, on the island of Cava, had a grandstand view of the drama:

As I sat upon my knoll, musing my childish thoughts and watching the cattle and arctic terns and the surrounding ships I saw a flag being hoisted on the flag halyards of the *SMS Friedrich der Grosse*, the ship nearest to the Calf of Cava. When the flag reached its highest point a light breeze caught it for a moment and it fluttered out, the iron cross and double eagle of Germany, then right behind it another red flag climbed the mast but no breeze stirred it. Like a piece of old rag it hung in shame. Then across

John Tulloch (1909–1974) in service uniform during the Second World War. (Leslie and Joyce Howard)

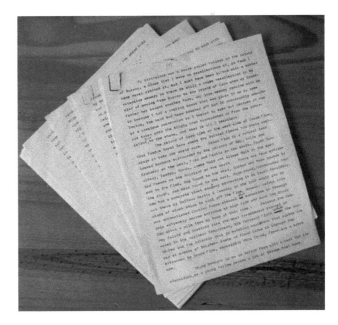

The original typescript of John Tulloch's account of the scuttling of the German fleet as he remembered it later in life. He lived on the island of Cava, and so had a grandstand view of the events of 21 June 1919. (Author's Collection)

Imperial German Naval Ensign from SMS *Moltke,* acquired after the scuttling. This was the flag that was hoisted just before the ships were scuttled. (National Maritime Museum, Greenwich)

the waters a bell began to ring, clang, clang, clang, at first I thought it was the church bell in the Auld Kirk of Orphir, but listening more keenly I could hear that it came from one of the ships, either the *Baden* or the *Bayern.*

From the Calf, where I sat on my knoll, the whole of Scapa Flow was within my view and as I gazed around from ship to ship I could see that they were all now either flying flags or in the act of hoisting them, and a great number of the ships were listing over to one side. Returning my gaze to the *Bayern* that was lying immediately in front of where I sat I could see that something most unusual was taking place aboard as she had now taken a dangerous list to the right. Many times before I had seen ships being listed over so that seaweed and barnacles could be scraped off their bottoms and at first this occurred to me, but as the *Bayern* kept listing further and further my mind panicked. "She has listed too far, they will never get her back." I thought. By this time I was standing up with excitement, then from the far side of the ship appeared two boats loaded with sailors; they headed straight for the Calf of Cava, their nearest shore right below where I was standing. I was rooted to the spot in fascination as the *Bayern* continued to list further and further until she at last dropped over on her side, hesitated for a few moments before turning upwards, then in slow motion the bows disappeared under the water, the stern shot up into the air and with a smother of foam and exploding bubbles of air she slid into the depths of Scapa Flow.

The battleship SMS *Bayern* sinking by the stern, 21 June 1919. (Imperial War Museum Photographic Archive)

For a while I stood in a daze watching fountains of water shoot up from where the *SMS Bayern* had disappeared. Then across the waters floated a German cheer, "hooch, hooch, hooch". Suddenly my senses returned; I looked around me and on every side battleships, cruisers and destroyers of the German High Seas Fleet were sinking and boat loads of German sailors were rowing towards Cava. Panic seized me and I commenced to high tail it for home; terror filled my young heart. It was bad enough to see huge battleships turn turtle and sink beneath the waves on every side but added to that to have boat loads of people that I had been taught to look upon as my enemy rowing towards my island home and nobody of my own clan within half a mile put wings on my heels, and like Mercury I tore down the peat track that led towards home.

On the *Flying Kestrel*, the first inkling that something unusual was happening was the sight of German sailors putting off from their ships in boats and rafts. The children then noticed that the big ships were lower in the water than they had been earlier. A passing drifter hailed the *Flying Kestrel*, with the message, 'The Germans are sinking their ships!', and told them to go back to the *Victorious* for further orders. A member of the crew, David Sutherland, noticed something else:

The German ensigns were being hauled up on the vessels, they bore what looked like an iron cross ... We could see German sailors running about their decks, shouting and making gestures at us, but on one of the biggest battleships – *Baden* it turned out to be – the only human being we could see was a sailor dressed in white, dancing a hornpipe on the foredeck. Nearby were some destroyers and on their decks German

The battleship SMS *Bayern* sinking by the stern, 21 June 1919. (Imperial War Museum Photographic Archive)

sailors were singing and dancing and playing accordions and other instruments. But for the fact that the ensigns were up and the vessels obviously being scuttled, it looked quite a gay and happy scene. We had forgotten the purpose of our trip and the children and their teachers crowded the rails to look at the strange scene.

Thirteen-year-old Leslie Thorpe recorded that as the *Flying Kestrel* returned to the *Victorious*,

We came alongside with such a bump! We were ordered back to Stromness, and the vessel was then to return to the *Victorious*. As we came back we saw one ship bottom up, others turning turtle, and a battlecruiser sinking by the stern, turning over, and rapidly going down.

Other children remembered particular details of the scuttling. William Groundwater saw sailors dragging their kit across the deck and throwing it into the boats. Rosetta Groundwater saw men with their hands up, and one man shot and falling overboard. Peggy Gibson retained a vivid picture of the sea boiling as ships turned turtle, great gouts of water and explosions of steam bursting all around, German sailors being swept into the water and clinging to rafts and boats. While some of the children were thrilled by these sights,

Peggy Gibson as a child. She was one of the Stromness schoolchildren on the *Flying Kestrel* and retained vivid memories of the chaos and excitement of that memorable outing. She is seated, surrounded by her sisters and brother. (Author's Collection)

thinking naively that it had all been laid on for their benefit, others were frightened and anxious, and reduced to tears. Peggy Gibson recalls: 'I remember feeling absolutely amazed that I was there and seeing something that seemed like a display staged for me. I could hardly believe my eyes.' While Winnie Thorpe, Leslie's nine-year-old sister, remembers bursting into tears, and her brother putting a protective arm around her. 'Never mind, Winnie,' he said. 'We are witnessing history.'

The children on the *Flying Kestrel* were certainly in potential danger themselves, as they were only a hundred yards away from these great warships as they sank. The *Seydlitz* turned turtle nearby, water pouring from her seacocks.

Peggy Gibson 'saw twelve capital ships sinking. Some stood on their bows, some went over on their sides and the water was boiling everywhere.'

The children also witnessed the shooting and violence that resulted from anger and panic amongst the few British ships on the scene at the time. Leslie Thorpe remembers that, 'one German boat was not showing the white flag, and the destroyer *Westcott* came up with her guns uncovered, and the men holding their rifles, ready for action. She fired on the boat with a machine gun and I heard that a man was killed.'

Len Sutherland (aged eleven) saw at least one German sailor shot on the deck of one vessel, 'but whether by a German or a British Officer I could not say ... There was fighting among the German sailors on some of the ships, and I shall always remember the scene that day.'

'The Scuttling of the German Fleet in Scapa Flow'. Illustration by Theo Matejko (1893–1946). Matejko was an Austrian painter and illustrator who in the Second World War became a leading propagandist for the Third Reich. Here he captures the chaos, and jubilation, as the German warship goes down with its ensign flying, and sailors jumping into the sea.

Peggy Gibson recalls: 'We came alongside a trawler that had been picking up German Officers for interrogation. They looked very bold. They were sitting ramrod straight and proud even though the British sailors were training guns on them.'

Kitty Watt, one of the senior schoolgirls, heard small arms fire too. She watched a drifter towing several boats full of German sailors, 'one of whom tried to cut the tow-rope and free his boat, whereupon one of the Marine guards on the drifter shot and killed him.'

According to both children and British naval officers, the scene was one of 'pandemonium with a strong dash of panic'.

Amidst all this it was hard work for Captain Davies to keep the *Flying Kestrel* head on to the turbulent waters as he zig-zagged back to Stromness. As they went through the boom defences they saw people on shore waving at them and the realisation dawned that those waiting and watching had been very concerned for them. The *Flying Kestrel* arrived back at Stromness about 2.30 p.m., and found the piers crowded with anxious parents and relatives, making the children feel very important as the only civilian eyewitnesses on the spot of the scuttling. Peggy Gibson remembers 'there was great distress in the town. My parents knew I was out there with my three sisters and every pier in Stromness was lined with people wondering if the boat with the bairns in would come back.'

The harbour at Stromness, from where the children from the Stromness Academy embarked on their trip on the *Flying Kestrel*. (Author's Collection)

With typical bathos, on their arrival home Peggy Gibson's older sister was more worried that her hat had blown off during the voyage and fallen into the Flow than she was about the momentous events she had witnessed. And Kitty Tait realised that in spite of having packed her favourite orange cream biscuits, they came back uneaten because of all the excitement.

Meanwhile, news that something extraordinary was happening in the Flow was already circulating on the Mainland. William Caldwell, who lived at Scapa, remembered a man on a bicycle pedalling furiously past his house, shouting something and pointing up the road.

We followed in his direction up the road until we came to a point overlooking Scapa Flow. There we saw an amazing sight. Those fine ships we had seen so recently were now in every possible state of confusion. All were sloping irregularly: some were already half-submerged. They were all listing wildly and even as we looked, one vessel turned over. We saw the gleam of reflected light from her dripping underside as it came up out of the water. Slowly and gently her funnels made one last farewell bow before they plunged beneath the waves. There arose a tremendous column of foam and spray, which at that distance, appeared solid and motionless for many long excited seconds. Then it flattened down and there was nothing. That mighty vessel had gone to the bottom.

There was an amusing element to the unfolding drama too. Kenneth Flett of Mussaquay was at a funeral in the Orphir kirkyard. The coffin had just been lowered when a whisper went round the mourners: 'Boy, the Germans are sinking their ships.' The Minister was in the middle of the committal with his eyes closed in prayer. When he opened his eyes he was shocked to find that the mourners had deserted the graveside and were lining the kirkyard dyke gazing at the amazing spectacle in the Flow.

Arthur Burnett, who had served in the Home Guard during the First World War, was now living at home at Grievehouse in Stenness and working as a farm labourer at a farm in Orphir whose land overlooked the Flow. This particular Saturday he had been singling neeps and was coming to the end of his morning's work when he looked up and saw several small boats leaving the German warships in the Flow. His granddaughter Sheena Taylor takes up the story:

James Burnett, Arthur's older brother, in the uniform of the Seaforth Highlanders standing near the steading at Grievehouse. He was killed at the Battle of Vimy Ridge. At the outbreak of the First World War Arthur had been deemed 'unfit for service' on a technicality: he was claiming to be a year older than he was in an attempt to enlist. Instead he was drafted into the Home Guard. He served on Fair Isle and later on Rousay, but after the end of the war came back to live with his parents at Grievehouse, working on a farm at Orphir. While out in the fields he saw strange things happening to the ships in the Flow, but could not believe the evidence before his eyes and retired to his bed, believing that he had sunstroke. Only later did he discover that he really had witnessed the German fleet sinking. (Sheena Taylor)

Grievehouse, where Arthur Burnett lived with his parents. (Sheena Taylor)

When he looked up again, some large ships seemed to be lower in the water, wavering unsteadily on the surface. He put the movement down to heat haze over the sea. Next time he lifted his eyes, some hulls appeared to have sunk even lower and, when he saw the stern of one seeming to rise high in the air, he was sure the sun on the back of his neck had got to him.

For one of the few times in his life he downed tools early to cycle home – very carefully. Once there, he lay down straight away, refusing the food his mother offered him. He was sure he'd had some sort of turn and was losing his wits. He said nothing to her about that, simply turning his face to the wall to sleep.

Later, in the afternoon, his mother wakened him with the astounding news the man with the horse-driven post cart had brought, that all the ships of the German Fleet were under the waves or beached on the shore. Several people on Hoy and around the Flow had seen the same incident, but Arthur claimed he was probably the only one who really did not believe his eyes. He claimed the food he accepted once he knew what had happened was the best-tasting meal he ever ate.

John Tulloch, having retreated to the safety of his parents' farm on the island of Cava, was able to observe the action from the roof of an outbuilding and saw the German fleet

Arthur Burnett and his family, Jean, Georgina (Moar) and Margaret, at Melsetter, Longhope, *c.* 1938. (Sheena Taylor)

vanishing beneath the waters of the Flow, although by now the few British ships present were making efforts to prevent at least some of the ships from sinking:

> Drifters were pulling at huge battleships like ants with large beetles. Two destroyers, the *Westcott* and the *Walpole*, were now tearing around the Flow blowing out anchor chains. The drifter *Clonsis* had the SMS *Dresden* in tow, but could not quite make it to Cava before it sank. The anchor chain of the SMS *Nürnberg* was somehow dropped and this ship drifted into the shore directly below my home on the island of Cava.
>
> The SMS *Seydlitz* was anchored in shallow water, therefore did not turn turtle like most of the others, she heaved over on her side and there she lay like a monster whale with one half above water. The Germans must have had pigs aboard as one swam away squealing in terror until it eventually cut its own throat with its front hooves.
>
> The SMS *Moltke* turned turtle near the island of Rysa Little but as she was also in fairly shallow water we could hear the masts and superstructure crunching as it broke with her weight bearing down upon them into the seabed. When she finally subsided her keel still showed above the water where it could be seen for some time afterwards, but she kept settling down until only her keel showed at low tide.

The *Seydlitz* capsized, with her propeller showing above the water. (Orkney Photographic Archive)

The SMS *Derfflinger* was anchored under the cliffs known as The Bring on the island of Hoy, and she made a great fuss about sinking. After listing over and over until she lay on her side then she turned turtle and her stern shot up into the air until she appeared to be standing on her bows, then she dived into the depths below, something aboard her exploded and fountains of water shot into the air, after a little while a second explosion sent more water rocketing out of the sea above her. The water around where she had vanished seethed and boiled for a long time after she had gone. She must have been a mighty Gladiator in battle and such an undignified death was hard to bear.

The SMS *Kaiser* turned over at a great speed. I was watching her turn over and saw a steam pinnace that was in the davits on her off side soar into the air; the fastening ropes broke and it somersaulted over and over slowly in the air before it dropped down into the sea right side uppermost and floated away to drift in below my home and lie on the rocks until my uncle later salvaged it.

No one in my family remembered anything about the time; we usually had dinner about twelve o'clock, but today we had no dinner. After the first hour of watching no German sailors came ashore although there were hundreds floating off-shore in their boats. My uncle ventured down to join the army corporal and his men who were patrolling the shore with loaded .303 rifles and shooting over the heads of any Germans who came too near the beach.

Scapa Flow June 21st 1919. Oil painting by Bernard Gribble (1920). Gribble was a marine painter on board the trawler *Sochisin* making drawings of the German ships when the scuttling took place. Here he records the scene when boats of German sailors showing white flags approach the British guard ship, having abandoned their sinking battleship. The German officer is asking to come aboard, but the British sailors with guns at the ready are telling him to return to his ship and stop it sinking. Gribble has effectively captured the tension and anger as the ships begin to capsize. (Harris Museum and Art Gallery, Preston, Lancashire.) (UK/Bridgeman Images and Nick Gribble)

Another civilian with a ringside seat was the marine artist Bernard Gribble (1872–1962), who was at Scapa making drawings of the German ships and had decided that morning to join the patrol trawler *Sochisin*, which was cruising around the German fleet. Gribble was at Scapa Flow as the Official Maritime Painter to the Worshipful Company of Shipwrights and was an accomplished painter of historical and maritime scenes noted for his meticulous research and close attention to details of the ships he painted. His paintings and drawings are a valuable contemporary record of the action in the Flow at the time of the scuttling. Gribble records:

At 11.45 am I noticed German sailors on the *Friedrich der Grosse* throwing baggage into boats lying alongside the vessel. I remarked to Lieutenant Leeth, "Do you allow them to go for joy rows?" He said "No", and then added "I've got it! I believe they are scuttling their ships." We made for the *Frankfurt*, and Leeth ordered the Germans back to their ship. The Germans shouted "We have no oars", whereupon a Petty Officer threw some into the sea calling out "There you are, you swine." Leeth told those approaching the

The Sinking of the German Fleet at Scapa Flow by Bernard Gribble. This is the second of two large oil paintings by Bernard Gribble, who was a marine artist up in Orkney to record the German ships, and on board the trawler *Sochisin* when the scuttling began. He described what happened in an article in the *Orcadian* newspaper. This picture captures the scene when German boats from the cruiser *Frankfurt* approached the trawler but were ordered at gunpoint to return to their ship to stop it sinking. (National Museums Scotland and Nick Gribble)

trawler in boats to return to their ships or he would fire on them, which he proceeded to do. Gribble recalls a German Officer waving a white flag and shouting: "You have killed four of my men and we have no arms. I want to look after my men." When the order to return to their ships was repeated the German Officer replied "We can't go back. They are sinking. It's not our fault. We are carrying out orders."

Gribble reported 'a good deal of cross-fire which lasted about three quarters of an hour.'

There were now many hundreds of men in the water, clinging to life rafts and in boats. Captain Robert Shaw, in command of a small patrol boat, remembers going to the battlecruiser *Seydlitz*, but just as they came alongside she turned turtle and nearly took his boat down too:

There were boatloads of Germans rowing about the anchorage. I was about to take them aboard when my rather wise Petty Officer said: "There are a lot more of them than there are of us, sir." So we towed them astern, four or five boats, and took them across to our big ships as they returned.

The cruiser *Frankfurt,* on the left, towed inshore and beached, while the *Baden* on the right is being stabilised, with British tugs around it. (Orkney Photographic Archive)

German sailors taking to the boats from sinking destroyers. (Orkney Photographic Archive)

The crew of a German destroyer taking to the boats. From an original photograph by C. W. Burrows. (Orkney Photographic Collection)

On HMS *Westcott*, one of the destroyers still in Scapa Flow, and now lying in Gutter Sound, Lieutenant Brian De Courcy-Ireland and fellow officers were having a gin before lunch when the senior sub-lieutenant burst into the wardroom and called out, 'The Germans are abandoning ship!' They thought he was joking at first but when they rushed up on deck they realised what was happening. Brian recalled that there was no way they could prevent seventy ships from being scuttled. However, the *Westcott* went at full speed towards the bigger ships to try to stop their crews from abandoning ship, firing their guns close to one of the cruisers, an action which merely caused the whole crew to jump over the side into the Flow.

The *Hindenburg* was not very far away, so Brian and the First Lieutenant with about twenty men boarded her. The crew had opened the sea cocks and abandoned ship, so with all power disconnected they had to work in pitch darkness to try to close the hatches. Meanwhile water was pouring in and the ship was gradually settling lower, so they climbed up to the bridge as the water covered the upper decks. In fact the *Hindenburg* settled upright on the bottom of the Flow and one of the whaling boats came alongside and took them off. Brian clearly remembered the sight that day. 'Everywhere we looked we saw mast after mast sticking out of the water, it was an awesome sight. An entire fleet of ships, ships that had fought at Jutland, all scuttled. We were the only warship to witness this extraordinary event...' (Quoted from *The True Glory: The Royal Navy 1914–1939*, Max Arthur, 1996)

Vice-Admiral Sir Robert Prendergast, Officer Commanding the Orkneys and Shetlands, in his subsequent report to the Admiralty on the events of that day, set out his immediate response to the crisis:

12.11 pm A message was sent summoning all available small craft to *Victorious*. they were despatched to round up crews and assist in the salvage work.

12.55 pm He was informed that Admiral Von Reuter was afloat in a trawler and that all German ships were being sunk.

1.30 pm A string of boats in tow of puffers began arriving at *Victorious* and the Destroyer Depot Ship *Sandhurst*. Prisoners were searched and assembled on the quarterdeck.

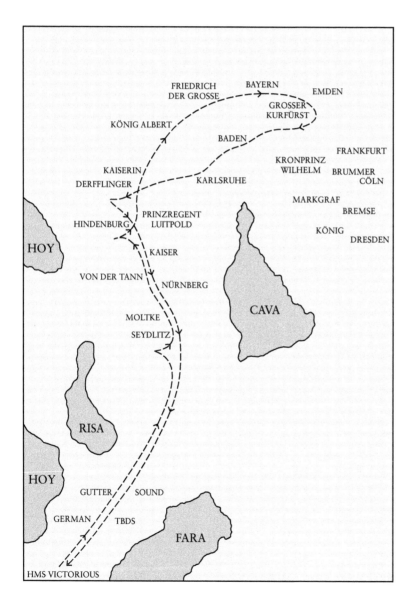

Journey taken by C. W. Burrows on the picket boat during the scuttling of the German fleet, with orders to board any German vessels still afloat and save the lives of the crew. (Author's Collection)

C. W. Burrows, who was Cashier of the Dockyard Section of the Naval Base between 1915 and 1920, made a comprehensive record of life at the base on Orkney, published as *Scapa and A Camera* in 1921, and gained permission from Vice-Admiral Prendergast to accompany him on an inspection of some of the sinking destroyers, to see if there was anything that could be done to save them.

We reached *Seydlitz* at about one o'clock, boarded her and hauled down her colours, and at the same time opened the windlass with a view to parting it and allowing the vessel to drift ashore, but unfortunately it brought up at the slip and held. The *Seydlitz* was then beginning to list heavily, so we left her and next boarded the *Hindenburg* which was also beginning to list heavily to port.

We then proceeded past several of the battleships, which were seen to be rapidly settling down. Whilst abreast of *König Albert* our picket-boat was hailed from the deck of a trawler by the German Admiral, Von Reuter, who asked us to save the crew of the *Bayern*, who were in the water. Two drifters which were nearby were accordingly ordered close to the *Bayern* for this purpose, and we proceeded in the same direction. Immediately afterwards the ship turned over to port, bottom up, and sank, whilst the crews of the boats cheered loudly and waved their caps.

We next headed for the *Derfflinger*, on the way sending back several boats of Germans to the *Victorious*. On the way back we passed the *Hindenburg* which had

The battlecruiser *Hindenburg*, being scuttled in Scapa Flow, 21 June 1919. Her forward compartments have flooded, but she remains more or less on an even keel. (Imperial War Museum Photographic Archive)

then settled on to an even keel with her masts and funnels showing, whilst the *Seydlitz* was then resting in shallow water on her starboard side, with her decks nearly vertical, and her port propeller just showing above the water.

Meanwhile a considerable number of the destroyers had been beached by tugs and other small craft, in addition to three cruisers, while the *Baden*, the only battleship saved, was still afloat, though very low in the water. On arrival at the *Victorious* we found the ship crowded with Germans, who, after examination, were sent to the Flagship *HMS Revenge*, which had by this time returned to the Flow from the Pentland [Firth].

At about 12.45 p.m. a signal had been sent to Vice-Admiral Sir Sydney Fremantle on board HMS *Revenge* alerting him to what was happening, and the 1st Battle Squadron returned from the Pentland Firth to Scapa Flow at top speed. Hester Scarth of Binscarth was at Swanbister and remembers seeing the British destroyers coming back at full speed, and 'simply tearing across the Flow throwing up tremendous bow waves.'

Prebendary G. L. Bourdillon, the Naval Chaplain on board HMS *Royal Sovereign*, climbed into the fore-top as the ship sped back to gain the best view:

A group of scuttled German destroyers lying in Gutter Sound, between Hoy and Fara in Scapa Flow, 21 June 1919. (Imperial War Museum Photographic Archive)

The German destroyer *S137*, scuttled in Gutter Sound. (Imperial War Museum Photographic Archive)

We steamed into the middle of the Flow and dropped anchor. Immediately scores of trawlers and other small craft surrounded us, towing boatloads of German officers and men, the boats flying the flag of truce. It was an extraordinary scene, so different from the usual quiet routine of the Flow. All around were sinking ships. Here was a light cruiser with a heavy list: there the huge side of a battlecruiser on her beam-ends showing above the surface: there the upturned bows of a destroyer cocked high in the air: farther off several destroyers aground with their decks awash – and all about were numbers of our destroyers, trawlers, and other vessels picking up German prisoners. In one or two places large white patches of foam showed where a ship had sunk.

It was 2.30 pm when we anchored. By 6 pm all that remained of the whole German Fleet were (as far as we could see) one battleship, one battlecruiser (sinking), three light cruisers (beached) and some destroyers! I made some pencil sketches, and then came down to see the prisoners coming aboard. Boatload after boatload, in they poured, officers and men, till we had *over 400* of them on board! They were quartered mostly in the batteries both sides. All the arrangements worked smoothly, but there wasn't much sleep for anyone last night.

British Boarding party alongside sinking German Destroyer, 21-6-1919

COPYRIGHT, C. W. BURROW

A British boarding party comes alongside a German destroyer with guns at the ready. From an original photograph by C. W. Burrows. (Orkney Photographic Collection)

Eighteen-year-old Sub-Lieutenant Edward Hugh Markham David on board the *Revenge* recorded his experiences in a letter to his mother, describing the day as 'perhaps the grimmest and certainly the most pathetic of the whole war.'

A good half of the German Fleet had already disappeared, the water was one mass of wreckage of every description, boats, carley floats, chairs, tables and human beings, and the *Bayern* the largest German battleship, her bow reared vertically out of the water was in the act of crashing finally bottomwards, which she did a few seconds later, in a cloud of smoke bursting her boilers as she went.

Some of the British destroyers began firing their guns at German anchor cables, hoping to set them adrift so that they could run ashore, but in most cases it was too late. The German destroyers were anchored closer to the shore and so touched the bottom very quickly, remaining only partly submerged. Bernard Gribble reported that he saw some of the German officers wearing frock-coats, with yellow kid gloves, and smoking cigars,

Scuttled German destroyer *G102* with salvage tug alongside. A sailor is seen jumping on the forward section while others prepare to abandon ship. (Imperial War Museum Photographic Archive)

in a remarkably self-composed manner. Discipline had been tightest among the torpedo boat destroyers, and this was reflected in the officers' bearing and pride in what they had managed to achieve under the very noses of the British.

Of the larger warships, the *Friedrich der Grosse* went down first at 12.16 p.m., the *König Albert* sank at 12.54 p.m., followed by *Brummer* (1.05 p.m.), *Moltke* (1.10 p.m.), and then in the following order:

1.15 p.m.	*Kronprinz Wilhelm*	Battleship
1.25 p.m.	*Kaiser*	Battleship
1.30 p.m.	*Grosser Kurfürst*	Battleship
1.30 p.m.	*Prinzregent Luitpold*	Battleship
1.30 p.m.	*Dresden*	Light Cruiser
1.50 p.m.	*Cöln*	Light Cruiser
1.50 p.m.	*Seydlitz*	Battlecruiser
2.00 p.m.	*Kaiserin*	Battleship
2.00 p.m.	*König*	Battleship
2.15 p.m.	*Von der Tann*	Battlecruiser
2.30 p.m.	*Bayern*	Battleship
2.30 p.m.	*Bremse*	Light Cruiser

The German cruiser SMS *Bremse* having turned turtle and lying on the seabed. (Orkney Photographic Archive)

2.45 p.m.	*Derfflinger*	Battlecruiser
3.50 p.m.	*Karlsruhe*	Light Cruiser
4.45 p.m.	*Markgraf*	Battleship
5.00 p.m.	*Hindenburg*	Battlecruiser

The light cruisers *Emden*, *Frankfurt* and *Nürnberg* were beached, while thirty-two torpedo boats were sunk, fourteen settled in shallow water and four were either beached or had their compartments flooded.

Only the battleship *Baden* was reached in time, and boarded by a party of sailors who managed to close the sea cocks and get the pumps going again. Lieutenant E. J. Goudy was a member of the boarding party from HMS *Ramillies*, and remembers the scene vividly:

The water was almost up to the floor plates and I could get no life in the diesel so I told the German lieutenant to start it and he looked blank and said: "No Inglis". So I said "Right – up on deck!" Cartwright shouted "How about the generator?" I told Cartwright I'd found two Huns below and this one pretended not to understand that I wanted him to start the diesel. Cartwright replied "Take him below and shoot him if he won't do it."

Down we went again. By this time the water was over the floor plates. I took my revolver out of the holster and pointed it at his head and said, "Go on, start up."

German destroyers ashore on the island of Fara. (Author's Collection)

He replied, in perfect English "I'm not going to start it for you, you can shoot me."
I said, "So you do speak English", and he replied, "Yes, perfectly."

I couldn't help admiring the man and I remember thinking "What would I do if in his position?" The water was rising and it was too late to start the engine, and I did not do my duty ... but I had an admiration for the man.

In spite of this the *Baden* was saved, while the *Hindenburg*, the newest battlecruiser of the German fleet, having had its anchor chain blown away by the guns of HMS *Westcott*, drifted down past the *Von der Tann* and ran onto a shoal where she settled down with her decks awash and her forward masts above the high tide mark.

Another boarding party went aboard the *Markgraf* and ordered the crew to close the sea cocks but the commanding officer, Captain Walther Schumann, refused. Despite the display of a white flag by Schumann himself there was a scuffle and Schumann was shot in the head and died. It was all to no avail as all hands had then to abandon ship and the *Markgraf* sank beneath the Flow.

The German perspective on the events of the scuttling can be found in the accounts of Friedrich Ruge (*Scapa Flow 1919: The End of the German Fleet*, trans. Derek Masters, Ian Allan, 1973), and of Vice-Admiral Ludwig Von Reuter (*Scapa Flow: Grave of the German Fleet*, published 1921, reissued 2005, Simon Mills Wordsmith Publications).

Von Reuter, in his account, did not mince his words in criticising the initial reaction of the British guard boats. He described how the boat attending the *Friedrich der Grosse*, when it realised that the battleship was sinking, 'with never a thought opened a wild fire

A boat with German sailors on board being captured and taken in tow by an RAF motor boat from Houton Seaplane Station. The officer seen standing in the middle of his men was armed with a large Mauser automatic pistol and Zeiss X12 glasses. (Imperial War Museum Photographic Archive)

on the unarmed, weaponless occupants of the boats, despite the fact that these held up white flags.' When the other boats realised what was happening, 'They lost their heads and raged blindly against everything that did not appear to them to follow the usual routine. A panic had broken out amongst them, into which the destroyers that had remained in harbour also joined.'

Von Reuter, having finally given the order to sink the *Emden*, waited for the valves and torpedo tubes to be opened and then embarked his crew on a dispatch boat which was waiting alongside. He comments that 'the acts of ferocity committed against the unarmed German crews, remove any English right to be indignant over German violators of the rules of war.' He decided to try to go ashore and see the Admiral commanding to get him to stop the firing. They landed in a rocky bay, probably at Houton, and were met by an angry young man (in fact the C.O. of the Naval Air Station) dressed in tennis clothes, who 'threw himself into a speed-boat lying ready for him and drove out of the bay.' Von Reuter's boat then ran onto a shoal and stuck fast until the tide re-floated it. They then made for the *Bayern* and took some of its men on board before it sank. 'Three cheers from the crew give her the tribute of honour on her last journey.' As Von Reuter's boat made its way across the Flow he saw

Germany's battle-cruiser Hindenburg resting on the bottom at Scapa Flow, and (right) another view of the same warship come to her ignominious end at the hands of those who had been compelled to yield her up to inglorious internment.

One of the German destroyers at the moment of capsizing.

Line of the interned destroyers sinking at their buoys.

Boatloads of German officers and men, with some of their belongings, coming alongside H.M.S. Ramillies after the scuttling of the interned Fleet, and (in oval above) part of the German crews of the sunken ships in a boat flying the white flag, making for safety on board the British ships.

SINKING OF THEIR INTERNED FLEET AT SCAPA FLOW BY FAITHLESS GERMANS, JUNE 21ST, 1919.

519

A page from the *Daily Sketch* entitled 'Sinking their interned fleet at Scapa Flow by Faithless Germans June 21st 1919', showing the *Hindenburg* sunk, destroyers capsizing, and boatloads of German sailors with some of their belongings coming alongside HMS *Ramillies* and being towed to other British ships. (Alamy Ltd)

German prisoners from the scuttled ships on the quarter deck of HMS *Ramillies*, 21 June 1919. (Imperial War Museum Photographic Archive)

'the English battleships appearing in the bay. They storm in at full speed, cleared for action with their 15-inch guns trained on the remains of my squadron. Now is the time to go to this English Admiral to get him to put an end to these acts of hostility.' As Von Reuter's boat steers towards the British flagship, other boats full of survivors are taken in tow. Alongside the flagship, HMS *Revenge*, a ladder is put over the side and Von Reuter climbs on board to be met by Vice-Admiral Sir Sydney Fremantle.

Sub-Lieutenant Edward Hugh Markham David was on the *Revenge* and described the dramatic scene:

As the German climbed wearily over the side there was a deadly hush on board. I was a few feet behind Von Reuter so heard every word. Fremantle was of course the picture of smartness in all his Admiral's trappings whilst Von Reuter dishevelled, wet and white as a sheet was quite the opposite – at first there was a pause, the German standing at the salute, then the following conversation:-

Fremantle: I presume you have come to surrender?
Von Reuter: I have come to surrender my men and myself [with a sweeping gesture towards the fast sinking ships] I have nudding else.
[Pause]

Admiral Ludwig Von Reuter and his staff being escorted aboard the British flagship after the scuttling of the German fleet. (Imperial War Museum Photographic Archive)

Von Reuter: I take upon myself the whole responsibility of this, it is nothing to do with my officers and men – they were acting under my orders.

Fremantle: I suppose you realise that by this act of treachery [hissing voice] by this act of base treachery you are no longer an interned enemy but my prisoner of war and as such will be treated.

Von Reuter: I understand perfectly.

Fremantle: I request you remain on the upper deck until I can dispose of you.

Von Reuter: May my Flag Lieutenant accompany me?

Fremantle: Yes, I grant you that.

After this tense exchange Von Reuter was taken to the Admiral's cabin under guard.

Later in his letter home David reflected on the invidious position of the British guard force. Even though the Germans were unarmed, it was the duty of the British to force the men back on board to close the valves. Because the terms of the Armistice had been broken the British regarded the 'treachery' of the Germans as sufficient warrant for using maximum force, but David was clearly uncomfortable about the situation and admired the bravery of the German crews in refusing to save their ships. In the twenty-first century we may feel outraged that the British fired on unarmed sailors escaping from their sinking ships, but that is to impose a modern morality on what had basically reverted to a situation of war. David, in his letter, implies that there were casualties on the British side too: 'We lost very few men, just one or two were knifed as they climbed aboard the German ships, by fanatics who had stayed behind.'

This assertion, if true, would suggest that in the panic and chaos of the moment, with tensions and frustration running high, acts of violence were perpetrated on both sides, which is difficult to justify with hindsight. What we do know is that there were many witnesses to indiscriminate shooting from small arms and machine guns, and that nine German sailors died of gunshot wounds received on 21 June. They were eventually buried at the cemetery at Lyness on Hoy, and the gravestones of eight of them can still be seen there. Sixteen more sailors were wounded. Half of the casualties, four dead and eight wounded, came from the torpedo boats of the Sixth Flotilla, who had received the signal to scuttle last, and so their crews were the last to abandon ship. They were fired on by the British destroyers *Vega* and *Vespa* and four drifters, and their crews were ordered at gunpoint to go back on board and turn off the valves.

Friedrich Ruge, in his account of the scuttling, lists those who died as follows:

1. Korvettenkapitan Walther Schumann, Commanding Officer, *Markgraf.*
2. Chief Petty Officer Hermann Dittman, *Markgraf.*
3. Yeoman of Signals Hans Hesse, *Bayern.*
4. Stoker Karl Bauer, *Kronprinz Wilhelm.*
5. Warrant Engineer Wilhelm Markgraf, Torpedo Boat *V126.*
6. Chief Engine-Room Artificer Gustav Funkrath, *V126.*
7. Chief Engine-Room Artificer Friedrich Beicke, *V126.*
8. Stoker Karl Funk, *V127.*
9. Engineer Apprentice Kuno Evertsberg, *Frankfurt.*

Their bodies lie in the remote and peaceful cemetery at Lyness, set apart from the Allied graves, a mute testimony to the extraordinary drama of that Midsummer's Day. Von Reuter recorded his personal gratitude in his account of the scuttling:

I am deeply moved and full of thankfulness towards my brave officers and their valiant men, who carried out the work ordered in such a brilliant fashion. All these wonderful ships and torpedo boats had sunk, sunk into the grave.

As Friedrich Ruge commented: 'Our power is broken but our pride stands good.'

By 6 p.m. that afternoon it was all over. The German High Seas Fleet had disappeared beneath the waters of the Flow, the last to go being the *Hindenburg*, whose masts and twin funnels sitting above the water line remained a visible marker of the sunken ships for twelve years afterwards. Drifters, tugs and destroyers could still be seen towing lines of small boats full of German sailors as they headed for the different ships of the 1st Battle Squadron to deliver up their prisoners.

The graves of the German sailors who lost their lives on the day of the scuttling, 21 June 1919, together with other German sailors who died in the First World War. A poignant group of graves lying in Lyness Cemetery, at a distance from the British section. (Author's Collection)

The battlecruiser SMS *Hindenburg* has by this stage settled on the bottom, with only her masts, funnels and the upper part of her superstructure showing. (Imperial War Museum Photographic Archive)

German destroyers aground on the island of Fara after scuttling. (Orkney Photographic Archive)

Ten-year-old John Tulloch on the island of Cava turned his attention to the jetsam that had floated ashore on the light western wind. He recalls:

I was in my glory dragging suitcases, kitbags and boxes out of the sea ... My uncle Harry had yoked one of our horses in a cart and we threw all our findings in until the cart was piled high with suitcases, kitbags, and boxes of all descriptions, but the shore was still littered with rafts, boats, lifebelts, crates and a thousand and one other things that had floated ashore. For days afterwards we collected everything that was useful and no one stopped us, even the army corporal and his men had their fair share.

When we had time to look over our treasures some of them proved to be treasures indeed, there were binoculars, typewriters, bottles of whisky, uniforms with gold braid, flags, chocolate, in fact thousands of things that were priceless. I had found a beautiful officer's dress sword in its scabbard and belt but my uncle spoke me out of it. For weeks afterwards I wore an officer's full dress cap that sat on top of my ears but it had all the gold braid and trimmings that befitted a high ranking officer.

There must have been many others living around the Flow who picked up souvenirs of the scuttling that day. The author was given a brass candleholder many years ago by

BRINGING OUT THE SOUVINERS.

A photograph entitled 'Bringing out the Souvenirs', showing two salvage workers displaying what they had discovered inside a scuttled German warship. (Orkney Photographic Archive)

Brass candle-holder salvaged from SMS *Hindenburg*, and now in the author's possession. Similar candle-holders can be seen in the displays at the Stromness Museum and the museum at Lyness. (Author's Collection)

a Stromness family friend, which originally came from the *Hindenburg*. Other similar candleholders can be seen in the museums at Stromness and Lyness, which house displays of assorted artefacts that were rescued from the German ships, either in the days after the scuttling or during the process of salvaging the wrecks. They offer a tantalising glimpse of life on board the ships, and give us a human perspective on those who were forced to endure a harsh existence far from home.

At the end of that extraordinary day there must have been many excited children being coaxed to bed, just as Admiral Von Reuter, after a game of piquet with his flag lieutenant, settled down in his bunk aboard the *Revenge*. Along with young islanders like John Tulloch, the children of the Stromness Higher Grade School (Stromness Academy) had been witnesses of one of the most historic days in the world's history, although they were probably too young to realise it at the time. The Stromness Academy log book proudly recorded the day:

21st June 1919

By kind permission of the Rear Admiral Commanding Orkneys and Shetlands the pupils and teachers were conveyed by HMS *Flying Kestrel* to view the German Fleet in Scapa Flow. They had the unique experience of seeing the ships afloat, sinking, and sunk, with the Imperial German Ensigns flying at the mastheads, as their crews apparently by general agreement had made up their plans to sink them on this date. The crews were seen in small boats, pinnaces, and rafts etc. By 4 pm only the *Baden,* a light cruiser ashore on the west of Cava, and the turrets of the *Hindenburg* were to be seen from the school.

Sailor's cap from SMS *Hindenburg*. (Stromness Museum Collection)

A pair of German fleet binoculars.
(Stromness Museum Collection)

Ship's bell from
SMS *Dresden*. (Stromness
Museum Collection)

Brass ship's clock, inscribed
'Th. Elbing' with a crown,
capital M and the number
1942. From an unknown
German ship. The hands
have stopped at ten minutes
past six. (Stromness
Museum Collection)

Brass binnacle from SMS *Bayern* and parts
from an unknown ship, amalgamated
to create this artefact. Reconstructed
at Hatson Youth Training Centre.
(Stromness Museum Collection)

Command Flag,
Imperial German Navy.
The flag was removed
from the *Hindenburg*
after the scuttling.
(National Maritime
Museum, Greenwich)

CHAPTER 3

Salvage

There were conflicting reactions to the events of 21 June 1919. Admiral Wemyss, one of the British delegation at Versailles, privately wrote: 'I look upon the sinking of the German Fleet as a real blessing. It disposes, once and for all, the thorny question of the redistribution of these ships.' Publicly, however, there was outrage that the scuttling had happened. *The Times* of 23 June 1919 called it 'this deed of stupid cunning and impotent arrogance.'

During the night of 21 June the British squadron sailed south for the Cromarty Firth, with the 1,774 German officers and men aboard. They arrived about midday, and when the ships had anchored Admiral Von Reuter and his staff were summoned to the *Revenge*, where they assembled on the quarterdeck on which a detachment of Royal Marines had fallen in, forming a square, carrying rifles with fixed bayonets. Admiral Fremantle faced Von Reuter and read out an address in which he expressed his indignation at the violation of the 'common honour and the honourable traditions of seamen of all nations.' He accused Von Reuter of a flagrant violation of the Armistice, and of a breach of faith and honour. He concluded, 'I now transfer you to the custody of the British military authorities as prisoners of war.'

Von Reuter, in his account of the meeting, says that he could only shake his head at what he suspected was a scene staged for the benefit of the British press and designed to deflect attention from the embarrassment felt by the British naval command. He replied in German:

> Tell your Admiral that I am unable to agree with the burden of his speech and that our understanding of the matter differs. I alone carry the responsibility. I am convinced that any English naval officer placed as I was would have acted in the same way.

Admiral Von Reuter was then taken south by train, and eventually arrived at the prisoner-of-war camp at Donington Hall in Leicestershire. He expected to face trial for ordering the scuttling of his fleet, and spent much time lobbying on behalf of his crews, and preparing his case. He knew that he was publicly despised by the British authorities and an object of considerable hostility to the majority of the British population.

A medal commemorating the scuttling of the German fleet, showing a bust of Admiral Ludwig Von Reuter and on the reverse a picture of a sunken ship. The inscription around the outside reads: 'God defend the third German Fleet', and around the bust of Admiral Reuter: 'Undefeated in her self-chosen grave: Vice Admiral Ludwig Von Reuter.' The sinking of the German fleet was greeted in Germany with jubilation, as it was felt that this act restored the honour not just of the German Navy but also the German people. When Von Reuter was released from captivity early in 1920 he travelled by sea to Wilhelmshaven, where he received a hero's welcome, with the head of the Admiralty, detachments of troops and inhabitants of the town all gathered on the quayside to welcome him home. (National Maritime Museum, Greenwich)

Among the German military command and the general population in Germany there was, by contrast, great admiration for the scuttling, and jubilation that the honour of Germany, humiliated by the conditions of the Treaty of Versailles, had been somewhat restored. Admiral Sheer was defiant:

I rejoice over the sinking of the German Fleet in Scapa Flow ... the stain of surrender has been wiped out from the escutcheon of the German Fleet. The sinking of the ships has proved that the spirit of the Fleet is not dead. This last act is true to the best traditions of the German navy.

(The Times, 1 July 1919)

All sorts of wild theories and accusations were bandied about concerning whether Von Reuter had acted on direct orders from Berlin. Much was made of the discovery of wreaths found in the ships which contained flowers not available in Orkney at the time, and therefore probably brought over from Germany in the last supply ship to arrive, two days before the scuttling. This was thought to suggest that there was a pre-arranged plan. In fact there is no evidence to suggest a conspiracy, and it is much more likely that, as he said, Von Reuter acted on his own initiative, basing his decision on the imperfect information he had, and the standing orders of the German Imperial Navy that no ship was ever to be given up to the enemy.

The people of Orkney were in no doubt that what had happened was for the best. The Hoy postmaster Isaac Moar summed up local feeling when he said: 'We were all glad he did what he did ... He did a good service to peace – and provided a lot of local employment later on!'

During the weeks immediately following 21 June the scuttled ships became a local tourist attraction. Thirteen-year-old Leslie Thorpe added as a postscript in his letter to his father:

As a kind of sequel, last Thursday [3 July 1919] we went to Kirkwall in a motor car, round by Houton Air Station and Swanbister or Smoogro Bay. The SMS *Baden* and *Emden* are lying beached at Swanbister Bay. We went right down to the shore to see them. The *Emden* is a light cruiser. They were pumping water out of her. On the shore I picked up some papers in German, most infernally badly written.

Henry Halcro Johnston, writing to his brother on 17 August 1919 from the Stromness Hotel, described how on 24 June he took a round trip from Stromness to Longhope and back on the steamship *Hoy Head*.

When we cleared Houton Head we saw the light cruiser *Bremen* lying on her side about 120 yards off Foyness ... The light cruiser *Nürnberg* was beached on the west side of Cava about half a mile south of the *Hindenburg*. Between the *Hindenburg* and the *Seydlitz* we saw the bottom of another ship above water at low tide ... The *Hoy Head* steamed between Ryssa Little and Muckle Ryssa and when we entered Gutter Sound we saw the tips of the masts of many sunken destroyers in the channel between Ryssa Little and Fara.

The *Baden, Emden, Frankfurt* and *Nürnberg* and eighteen destroyers had been beached before they could sink. However, ten battleships, five battlecruisers, five light cruisers and thirty-two destroyers were successfully scuttled and sunk, fifty-two out of the seventy-four ships that had steamed into the Flow in November 1918. The Admiralty quickly decided that they should be left where they had sunk. But some of the submerged hulks were creating a hazard for local shipping, and occasionally trawlers found themselves beached on the wrecks. There was local protest in the press and a local salvage company, the Scapa

German destroyer *G40* beached at Mill Bay with the salvage boat alongside during salvage operations at Scapa Flow, 29 July 1925. (Imperial War Museum Photographic Archive)

Flow Salvage & Shipbreaking Company, began work, soon followed by Ernest Cox, a scrap metal merchant from the Isle of Sheppey, who in 1924 purchased twenty-six destroyers and the battlecruisers *Seydlitz* and *Hindenburg* from the Admiralty for £24,000.

Over the next few years, through dogged determination and hard work, Cox managed to raise twenty-six destroyers, two battlecruisers and five battleships. The story of this heroic enterprise has been fully documented in two books, *The Man Who Bought a Navy* by Gerald Bowman, London, 1964, and *Jutland to Junkyard* by S. C. George, Cambridge, 1973. Cox began by raising the destroyers, and then moved on to the *Hindenburg*. However, this 27,000-ton battlecruiser was a much more difficult proposition. After three futile attempts to raise her Cox had to admit temporary defeat, but he then defiantly transferred his attentions to the *Moltke*, which lay in over 70 feet of water off the western side of the island of Cava.

Cox believed that the best way to raise these big ships was by sealing up all the openings in the hull and pumping in compressed air to force the water out and make the ship rise to the surface. In order to control the process, he decided to divide the interior of the *Moltke* into three sections which could then be separately filled with as much air as was needed. This entailed considerable risk for the salvage crews, who had to work in appalling conditions 50 feet beneath the surface.

John Tulloch, who as a boy had witnessed these ships being scuttled, after the war took a job with Cox & Danks, and became an acetylene cutter. He describes in his memoir what he had to do:

> Once the divers had fixed the airlocks and the air lines, a number of compressors were started up and pumped air into the now sealed hull to force the water level down. But it was soon discovered that there was more to it than just pumping air into a hull to raise it off the seabed.

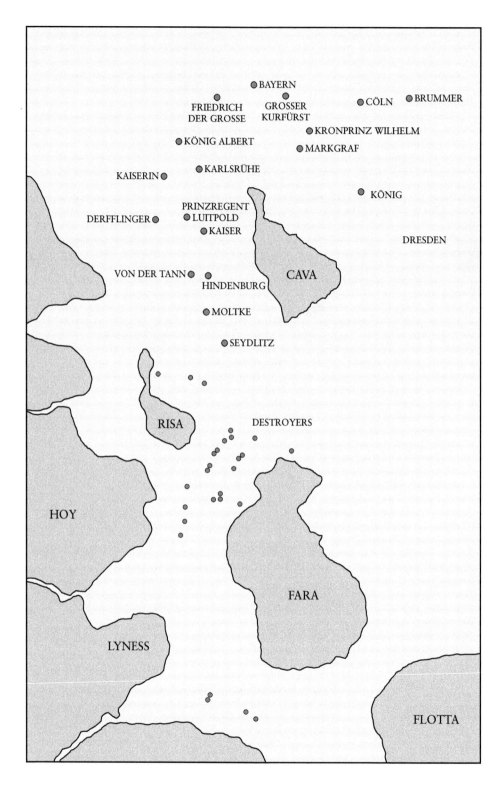

Map showing the position of the German fleet after scuttling. (Author's Collection)

The SMS *Hindenburg* in the process of being salvaged. (Orkney Photographic Archive)

Scuttled German ships with the salvage pontoon in the foreground. (Imperial War Museum Photographic Archive)

Thousands of tiny holes were discovered, which had to be patched up from the inside by gangs of acetylene cutters.

The pressure made their ears crack going down and up.

Inside the wreck there was a wilderness of oil-covered machinery, pipes, companionways and other obstructions all topsy-turvy as, of course, the ship was bottom side up.

Day by day we burned, cut and patched, all the time getting further into the bowels of the ship. The realisation that the sea was being held back all around us by the hull of the ship only made things very eerie at times.

If something went wrong there was not much chance of escape except when one was near the air locks.

John recalled one occasion when working away sealing the hull into three sections.

We had been working for about an hour when the electric light bulbs commenced to become hazy as if they were being steamed up. I stopped what I was doing and gazed around. Someone started yelling, "drop tools and run for the airlock." I had already dropped everything and commenced to make for the lock, the lights start to flicker until they gave one final flicker and went out.

Darkness descended and John stumbled, with outstretched arms, on to a manhole. 'A gale force wind tore through it and swept me with it, men were shouting everywhere, suddenly there was a movement in the hull and I sprawled on my face among the wreckage.'

Clawing himself upright, he reached for his torch, just as he was swept off his feet again by another gust and smashed against a bulkhead. Old pipes and other pieces of metal tore at his suit and gashed his hands and face.

John says he was 'crying like a child' at this point.

Just then the lights went on again and we all saw where we were. The air lock entrance was near and everyone raced for it, willing hands helping one another in until a count of heads showed that we were all there.

The hatch was smartly closed and the valve opened to let the air out. When we eventually got out of the lock and looked at each other we could not help laughing.

The men were black, apart from the whites of their eyes and teeth, and their clothes were tattered and torn. (*The Orcadian*, 15 September 2011)

Eventually, on 10 June 1927, the *Moltke* was brought to the surface and towed to Lyness, where she was fully sealed up and taken to Rosyth to be broken up. The next ships to be raised were the *Seydlitz* and the *Kaiser*, followed by the light cruiser *Bremse*. After these successful operations Cox was determined to return to the *Hindenburg*, and in July 1930, by using two destroyers filled with concrete as underwater wedges against the hull of the 27,000-ton battlecruiser, he successfully lifted her off the seabed and floated her on an even keel.

Emboldened by this success Cox turned his attention to the battlecruiser *Von der Tann*, which he raised by December 1930, and the 25,000-ton battleship *Prinzregent Luitpold*,

Two photographs showing the *Hindenburg* being raised, with water being pumped out of the superstructure.

which was raised the following year. However a combination of the onset of the Depression, and the death of an employee in a mysterious explosion on the *Prinzregent Luitpold*, caused Ernest Cox finally to withdraw from the salvage work at Scapa Flow.

Cox sold his remaining interest in the fleet to the Alloa Shipbreaking Company which, under the name of Metal Industries Ltd, went on to raise a further five ships before the outbreak of the Second World War brought operations to a halt.

The salvage operation generated a lot of interest both locally and nationally, and inspired a novel called *The Man from Scapa Flow* (published by Hodder & Stoughton in 1933) by Captain Henry Taprell Dorling (1883–1968), who served in the Navy during the First World War and wrote under the name 'Taffrail'. The plot revolves around the attempt of a German naval officer, Herman Bauer, to recover valuable material (jewellery and a stamp collection) from a safe inside the battleship *Prinzregent Rudolf*, a fictitious variant on the real *Prinzregent Luitpold*. A retired British naval officer, John Stafford, asked to go as a journalist to Orkney to report on the salvage work, becomes the sleuth who goes after this man Bauer who has been causing mayhem among the salvage company's men and equipment, and the novel ends with a thrilling chase across the island of Hoy, until

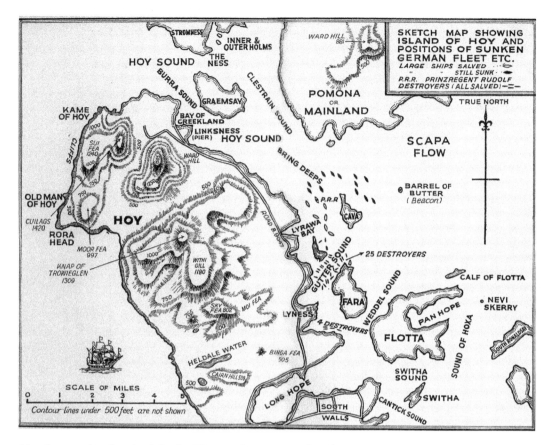

Sketch map showing the island of Hoy and positions of sunken German Fleet, from *The Man from Scapa Flow*, by 'Taffrail', Hodder & Stoughton, 1933. The *Prinzregent Luitpold* is renamed *Prinzregent Rudolf* in the novel. (Author's Collection)

the German sailor throws himself over the 600-foot cliffs facing the Atlantic Ocean. The novel gives a good summary of the scuttling, and contains much detail about the salvage operation. Because of his naval background 'Taffrail' could write with great authenticity about his subject, including diagrams in the text and a detailed map of Scapa Flow as a front endpaper. The author knows of no other representation in fiction of the events of that momentous day and the subsequent salvage operation, until the publication of *The Redeemed* by Tim Pears (Bloomsbury, 2019).

The seven wrecks that still remain at the bottom of the Flow, the battleships *Kronprinz Wilhelm*, *Markgraf* and *König*, and the light cruisers *Dresden*, *Cöln*, *Karlsruhe* and *Brummer*, are now scheduled under the Ancient Monuments and Archaeological Areas Act 1979, and lie on the bottom in depths of up to 45 metres. Because of their presence on the seabed, Scapa Flow has become one of the world's top diving destinations, offering a range of diving locations in relatively benign conditions, and providing a substantial boost to the local economy.

But more importantly and poignantly, these sunken ships, together with the little cluster of German graves at Lyness, are mute testimony to that extraordinary day 100 years ago, the greatest single loss of shipping in maritime history.

A study of the former German battlecruiser *Baden,* listing and under fire as a gunnery target in 1921. (Watercolour by William Wyllie) The *Baden* had been beached in Swanbister Bay, but was successfully salvaged. She was not broken up but was finally sunk by the Royal Navy as a gunnery target off Portsmouth on 16 August 1921. (National Maritime Museum, Greenwich)

The *Emden* or *Nurnberg* in Scapa Flow after being refloated in 1919. (Watercolour by William Wyllie) He has simply entitled it *Hun Cruiser.* There is a steam yacht moored alongside her, and more warships in the background. (National Maritime Museum, Greenwich)

A 150 mm deck gun from SMS *Bremse*, which had been scuttled in Cava Sound, dragged to Toy Ness and grounded. It was towed to Lyness by Cox & Danks and broken up there in 1929. The gun is at the entrance to the Lyness Naval Museum. (Author's Collection)

The events of 21 June 1919 were never forgotten by those who witnessed them. When interviewed for a magazine article in her eighty-fifth year, Peggy Gibson said:

> I still think about it. It was really remarkable, and not something anyone could easily forget, seeing those great ships first listing, then sinking, with a great roar of steam escaping, and the German sailors jumping into the water.

100 years on, there are no witnesses to the scuttling still alive. But, through the memories and records they left behind, the drama, chaos and terror of that fateful day can be vividly recreated for later generations for whom the scuttling of the German High Seas Fleet is simply part of distant history. Young Leslie Thorpe called his outing on the *Flying Kestrel* with his sister and schoolmates 'a most thrilling experience', and in a PS to his long letter to his father describing their adventures, added: 'Don't you think I'd better write a book about the scuttling of the German Fleet!'

Over the succeeding years a number of accounts have indeed been written, and a century later this account of that one momentous day, Saturday 21 June 1919, fulfils that young boy's aspiration, and tells this dramatic story afresh, through the eyes of those who saw it happen. As the young Leslie Thorpe said to his sister Winnie at the time: they were indeed 'witnessing history'.

A cluster of German graves at the Naval Cemetery at Lyness on Hoy, showing the last resting place of Walther Schumann, and Wilhelm Markgraf. (Author's Collection)

Peggy Gibson, who retained lifelong memories of seeing the scuttling of the German fleet as a ten-year-old girl, when part of the school party aboard the *Flying Kestrel*. Photograph taken in 1989 for the *Scotland on Sunday Magazine* by Richard Ansett.

Leslie and Winnie Thorpe with their parents, a photograph taken the year of the scuttling. (Author's Collection)

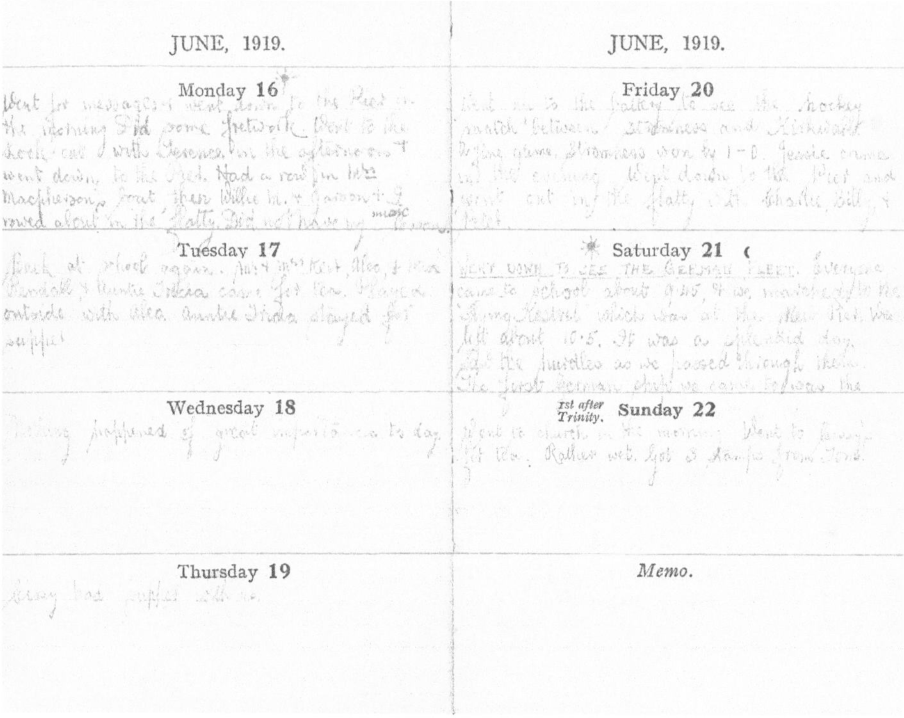

JUNE, 1919.

Monday 16

[handwritten diary entry, partially legible] Went for messages & went down to the Pier in the morning. Did some fretwork. Went to the Lock-out? with Terence in the afternoon & went down to the Uyet. Had a row in the? Macpherson, but then Willie M. & Gordon & I rowed about in the flatty. Did not have any more

Tuesday 17

[handwritten diary entry, partially legible]

Wednesday 18

[handwritten diary entry, partially legible] Nothing happened of great importance to day

Thursday 19

[handwritten diary entry, partially legible]

JUNE, 1919.

Friday 20

[handwritten diary entry, partially legible]

Saturday 21

[handwritten diary entry, partially legible] WENT DOWN TO SEE THE GERMAN FLEET. Everyone came to school about 9.15...

Sunday 22 _1st after Trinity._

[handwritten diary entry, partially legible]

Memo.

The diary of Leslie Thorpe, open at the page for 21 June 1919. He continued his account in the back pages of the diary. (Author's Collection)

The plot in Lyness Naval Cemetery on Hoy containing the graves of German sailors who were killed during the scuttling on 21 June 1919. (Author's Collection)

Postscript

View looking east down Scapa Flow from above the Bay of Houton, site of the wartime air station. (Author's Collection)

The Atlantic, restless, nudges the western crags,
Till Yesnaby, Hoy, Marwick
Are loaded with thunder, laced with spindrift.
Twice a day, ebb and flow,
Its slow pulse beats through the sounds
Till the islands brim like swans,
Till the islands lie in their seaweed like stranded hulks,
You would not think this grey, empty stretch
Where fishermen haul their creels
Sheltered the British Navy in two great wars,
And after the first holocaust
Imprisoned the Kaiser's warships
Until the prisoners opened their veins and drowned.

(From 'The Winter Islands' by George Mackay Brown, quoted in *Scapa Flow*, Malcolm Brown and Patricia Meehan, Allen Lane, 1968)

A view of Scapa Flow from the Hill of Midland at Orphir, looking across to the islands of Cava, Fara, Rysa Little and Flotta. This was the part of the Flow where the German fleet was interned. (Author's Collection)

APPENDIX

The Fate of the German High Seas Fleet

Name	Type	Sunk/Beached	Fate
Baden	Battleship	Beached	Transferred to British control, sunk as a target in 1921
Bayern	Battleship	Sunk 14:30	Salvaged September 1933
Friedrich der Grosse	Battleship	Sunk 12:16	Salvaged 1937
Grosser Kurfürst	Battleship	Sunk 13:30	Salvaged April 1938
Kaiser	Battleship	Sunk 13:25	Salvaged March 1929
Kaiserin	Battleship	Sunk 14:00	Salvaged May 1936
König	Battleship	Sunk 14:00	Unsalvaged
König Albert	Battleship	Sunk 12:54	Salvaged July 1935
Kronprinz Wilhelm	Battleship	Sunk 13:15	Unsalvaged
Markgraf	Battleship	Sunk 16:45	Unsalvaged
Prinzregent Luitpold	Battleship	Sunk 13:30	Salvaged March 1931
Derfflinger	Battlecruiser	Sunk 14:45	Salvaged August 1939
Hindenburg	Battlecruiser	Sunk 17:00	Salvaged July 1930
Moltke	Battlecruiser	Sunk 13:10	Salvaged June 1927
Seydlitz	Battlecruiser	Sunk 13:50	Salvaged November 1929
Von der Tann	Battlecruiser	Sunk 14:15	Salvaged December 1930
Bremse	Cruiser	Sunk 14:30	Salvaged November 1929
Brummer	Cruiser	Sunk 13:05	Unsalvaged
Cöln	Cruiser	Sunk 13:50	Unsalvaged
Dresden	Cruiser	Sunk 13:30	Unsalvaged
Emden	Cruiser	Beached	Transferred to French control, broken up in 1926
Frankfurt	Cruiser	Beached	Transferred to American control, sunk as a target in 1921
Karlsruhe	Cruiser	Sunk 15:50	Unsalvaged
Nürnberg	Cruiser	Beached	Transferred to British control, sunk as a target in 1922
S32	Destroyer	Sunk	Salvaged June 1925

S36	Destroyer	Sunk	Salvaged April 1925
G38	Destroyer	Sunk	Salvaged September 1924
G39	Destroyer	Sunk	Salvaged July 1925
G40	Destroyer	Sunk	Salvaged July 1925
V43	Destroyer	Beached	Transferred to American control, sunk as a target in 1921
V44	Destroyer	Beached	Transferred to British control, broken up in 1922
V45	Destroyer	Sunk	Salvaged 1922
V46	Destroyer	Beached	Transferred to French control, broken up in 1924
S49	Destroyer	Sunk	Salvaged December 1924
S50	Destroyer	Sunk	Salvaged October 1924
S51	Destroyer	Beached	Transferred to British control, broken up in 1922
S52	Destroyer	Sunk	Salvaged October 1924
S53	Destroyer	Sunk	Salvaged August 1924
S54	Destroyer	Sunk	Partially salvaged
S55	Destroyer	Sunk	Salvaged August 1924
S56	Destroyer	Sunk	Salvaged June 1925
S60	Destroyer	Beached	Transferred to Japanese control, broken up in 1922
S65	Destroyer	Sunk	Salvaged May 1922
V70	Destroyer	Sunk	Salvaged August 1924
V73	Destroyer	Beached	Transferred to British control, broken up in 1922
V78	Destroyer	Sunk	Salvaged September 1925
V80	Destroyer	Beached	Transferred to Japanese control, broken up in 1922
V81	Destroyer	Beached	Sunk on the way to the breakers
V82	Destroyer	Beached	Transferred to British control, broken up in 1922
V83	Destroyer	Sunk	Salvaged 1923
V86	Destroyer	Sunk	Salvaged July 1925
V89	Destroyer	Sunk	Salvaged December 1922
V91	Destroyer	Sunk	Salvaged September 1924
G92	Destroyer	Beached	Transferred to British control, broken up in 1922
V100	Destroyer	Beached	Transferred to French control, broken up in 1921
G101	Destroyer	Sunk	Salvaged April 1926
G102	Destroyer	Beached	Transferred to American control, sunk as a target in 1921
G103	Destroyer	Sunk	Salvaged September 1925
G104	Destroyer	Sunk	Salvaged April 1926

B109	Destroyer	Sunk	Salvaged March 1926
B110	Destroyer	Sunk	Salvaged December 1925
B111	Destroyer	Sunk	Salvaged March 1926
B112	Destroyer	Sunk	Salvaged February 1926
V125	Destroyer	Beached	Transferred to British control, broken up in 1922
V126	Destroyer	Beached	Transferred to French control, broken up in 1925
V127	Destroyer	Beached	Transferred to Japanese control, broken up in 1922
V128	Destroyer	Beached	Transferred to British control, broken up in 1922
V129	Destroyer	Sunk	Salvaged August 1925
S131	Destroyer	Sunk	Salvaged August 1924
S132	Destroyer	Beached	Transferred to American control, sunk in 1921
S136	Destroyer	Sunk	Salvaged April 1925
S137	Destroyer	Beached	Transferred to British control, broken up in 1922
S138	Destroyer	Sunk	Salvaged May 1925
H145	Destroyer	Sunk	Salvaged March 1925